"A valuable addition to any library"—*Booklist*

This eighth completely revised and updated edition, with its wealth of new data, is required reading for those who want complete information about collecting, selling, and evaluating foreign coins. Since its first publication almost thirty years ago, FELL'S INTERNATIONAL COIN BOOK has been the standard reference work that gives the most up-to-date price information on old and rare coins, as well as on coins currently in circulation.

FELL'S INTERNATIONAL COIN BOOK provides details on:

- coin denominations for over 200 countries
- how to evaluate foreign coins
- how to start a coin collection
- how to sell coins
- how to speculate and/or invest in coins
- how to recognize counterfeit coins
- how to clean, store, and exhibit coins
- a short history of coinage

And many other indispensible facts about collecting and selling foreign coins!

You'll find over 320 illustrations to aid in coin identification, as well as a fascinating history of coinage dating back to the ancient Greeks, and a list of magazines devoted to numismatics. All the information a collector needs is thoroughly explained so that the art of coin collecting and trading can be practiced intelligently and profitably. With increasing interest in collecting foreign coins, no collector can afford to be without this handy and unique reference book.

You will also enjoy FELL'S UNITED STATES COIN BOOK, Tenth Revised Edition.

For complete catalog write to: Frederick Fell Publishers, Inc.
386 Park Avenue South, New York, New York, 10016

$9.95

ISBN   0-8119-0587-X

S0-ACQ-397

FELL'S

INTERNATIONAL

COIN BOOK

EIGHTH REVISED EDITION

By
CHARLES J. ANDREWS

author of
Fell's U.S. Coin Book

FREDERICK FELL PUBLISHERS, Inc.   *New York*

International Standard Book Number: 0-8119-0595-0 (Cloth)
0-8119-0588-8 (Paper)
Library of Congress Catalog Card Number: 82-642107

For information address:

Frederick Fell Publishers, Inc.
386 Park Avenue South
New York, New York 10016

Published simultaneously in Canada by Fitzhenry & Whiteside, Limited, Toronto

Manufactured in the United States of America
1 2 3 4 5 6 7 8 9 0

Contents

Preface to Revised Edition

A STATEMENT FROM THE PUBLISHER

When this book was first presented years ago, its purpose was to cover the world's fastest growing hobby in compact, readable style. Since then great events literally shook the world. New nations were formed and tremendous numbers of new coins were minted. Other nations changed their types of coinage and metals used.

Now that coinage has reached unparalleled volume and diversification, this new, completely revised and up-to-date edition with its wealth of new data is a must for coin collectors everywhere. As a result of direct contact with informed correspondents throughout the world, it has been possible to quote old coins at their most recent and in some cases fantastic values along with the newer coinages that are due for similar climbs.

Beginning coin hobbyists will find full information for the identification of odd and strange looking foreign coins as well as other basic data. Advanced collectors will be pleased by the inclusion of many new items.

What is probably the most famous feature of FELL'S INTERNATIONAL COIN BOOK is the inclusion of a guide that enables the reader to quickly and easily identify the country of origin of each coin of the world.

So greatly has the field increased in the past few years that the preparation of this book has become a new and original task in itself. It is with a sense of real pride that this completed volume is presented to the coin collectors of the world.

Introduction

Numismatics is the science of coins and moneys. The name comes from the Latin word *numisma* meaning money. Students of government, religions or customs of various peoples can learn a good deal from observing coins. The pleasure of collecting them is so great that most of us who begin this activity retain an interest in it all the rest of our lives.

It is an unusual hobby because it is a source of profit rather than an expense and, being an intellectual pursuit, it also furnishes abundant pleasure. The thrill of adding to your collection elusive coins for which you have searched far and wide cannot be matched by any other experience.

The collecting of foreign coins and coins of antiquity is a separate field which allows full play of the imagination and challenges the skill of a collector. The romance of coins includes their historical value, their design and their mintage, but also far more. In 1893 Charles T. Tatmann, in the second report of the American Numismatic Association, wrote:

> The great majority of persons who gather these specimens of metallic ink do so because they are interested in the events thereby recorded. A youth who forms a collection learns the habits of close observation and accurate description; moreover, he becomes a lover of completeness and method in arrangement. He is easily led to the doors of a host of refining studies, and enters with eagerness. Numismatics illustrates history, chronology, mythology, geography, art, and philosophy—to all of which it is inseparably linked.

The refinement or barbarity of the peoples of the earth has been shown with fidelity by their coins. Some coins found in Asia a few years ago threw valuable historical light on the great Bactrian civilization of ancient Persia, of which very little had previously been known. And the gradual enlightenment of the British people during the last thousand years can be clearly observed by comparing the rudely stamped coins of the early Anglo-Saxons with those issued by the long succession of kings and queens, including the beautiful pieces which bear the likeness of Queen Victoria, on to those of Queen Elizabeth II.

As Tatmann said:

> In order to get the full value of your hobby, be sure that you read while you collect. Never let a coin lie in your collection until you can tell the history of it or at least connect it with some historical event. Be careful that your collecting does not drift into mere curiosity—let it rather be a constant incentive to further study of history.

Throughout this book you will see indications of the retail value of certain coins and types of coins which are worth (if you sell them) on an average about sixty percent of the prices indicated. That is to say, you may reasonably expect a dealer to pay about sixty percent of the price for which he can sell a coin.

There are many foreign coins of extreme rarity, but they cannot all be discussed in a book of this size. Just keep in mind that the age of a coin has nothing to do with its value; many old coins exist in tremendous quantity, while some modern coins are rare. Naturally those which are difficult to acquire are the ones for which a collector is willing to pay more.

The purpose of this volume, like its companion, *Fell's United States Coin Book,* is to give the reader basic information not only regarding rare coins, but those which are commonly in use today, along with their current price trends. Thus it not only fulfills its purpose as a guide, but serves as a compact catalog as well.

With the increasing interest in the collecting of foreign coins, many such items are being offered for sale not only by reliable dealers, but by issuing nations as well. Every serious collector is sure to come in contact with such channels, and thus become acquainted with the latest price lists and catalogs.

Hence he will find this guide always new and ever handy in its discussion and descriptions of coins in general, a source of ready reference that is unique in its field, as the constant demand for this volume had proven.

CHAPTER 1

What Are Coins?

Money became necessary long before recorded history, because men found it desirable to exchange the products of their labor. Even 8000 years ago the Chinese used money, but of course the invention of coins came much later. In Chapter 5 you will read about many of the things that were used as money in primitive days.

As soon as metal came into use as money, it was so much more convenient to handle that it quickly replaced other mediums of exchange. Barter, the direct way of exchanging commodities, was cumbersome, and men welcomed a chance to buy and sell more easily. At first metal was weighed every time it was used in a transaction, and later it was portioned in small lumps. Eventually it became the custom to stamp a piece of metal with a wedge-shaped die that indicated its worth. This was probably a development of the very old method of sealing, and before long the name of that wedge-shaped die was used for the money made with it— coin. When there was an inscription on the coin, it was not necessary to weigh it every time a purchase was made, for people knew the stamping proved how much this particular piece of metal was worth.

The ancient Lydians (who lived in the west part of Asia Minor eight centuries before the Christian era) coined money of electrum, which is a mixture of gold and silver as mined from the earth. Their coins were stamped with the symbol of the State and were issued in various weights, often showing the picture of some sacred object. Their emperor, Croesus, known in fable for his great wealth, was the first sovereign ever to use real gold for coinage. About 560 B.C. he issued coins which showed the heads of a lion and a bull facing each other and the Reverse showed an incuse square.

Stater of Lydia (Electrum), 660 B.C., worth $15

The right to coin money has always been and still remains the surest mark and announcement of sovereignty. For instance, many of the Mahometan coinages in India are said to have constituted merely a numismatic declaration of conquest. And in ancient Persia, whenever a new king ascended the throne, all the money in the royal treasury was recoined with his effigy.

As a consequence of a government's monopolizing the right to mint its own money, the State naturally assumed the responsibility of deciding what constituted money and what it was worth.

Now it is generally recognized that a coin is a piece of metal impressed with the symbol of a responsible government which guarantees its weight and quality for use in public exchange of goods and services. Such a coin is inscribed with the name of the government issuing it and with the amount of its value. Commemorative coins, however, are issued to celebrate special occasions or to show respect for certain citizens. Both types have their place in a collector's cabinet.

CHAPTER 2

How Coins Are Made

The making of coins belongs to the State. In ancient times many Greek cities were independent communities and each of them coined its own money. At other times large areas of the earth have been controlled by one political power, and in that case fewer types of coins have been issued.

Syracuse Decadrachm, about 300 B.C., worth $800

Persia, 400–300 B.C., worth $10

Macedon, 280 B.C., worth $10

Alexander, about 300 B.C., worth $8

In early days the impression on a coin was made by placing a piece of blank metal on points arranged in design and then striking the metal with a hammer. Another method was to mix the metal to the required standard, then hammer it down to the required thickness and roughly shape its edges with shears.

An early tool for stamping the inscription on blank discs was a pair of tongs, on both points of which a die was cut. Pressure by such tongs assured the stamping of a coin on both sides evenly. It was a long time before a coin press was contrived to facilitate this work.

In 1836 steam power became available and the press was gradually improved.

A milling press of today can mill in one hour as many pieces as several men used to mill in one week when the work had to be done by hand with screw presses. Prior to the Machine Age coins struck by hammer were usually irregular. Only machinery has made it possible to turn out coins with exact edges.

A Very Early Mint

Before the metal is ready for minting, it must be assayed, weighed, melted, then poured into molds of the proper size. After the ingots have been tested for correct weight, they are taken to the cutting machines, where the coin blanks (or planchets) are cut by means of a steel punch working in a matrix. These planchets are cleaned of grease, rinsed in water and dried in large copper pans. Next, at sorting tables all those that are underweight ("lights") are thrown out to be remelted, while those above legal weight ("heavies") are filed down. During the milling process the raised rim is produced around the edge to protect the surface from abrasion.

There is always one die for the upper and another for the under side of a coin. A cylinder of steel is turned in a lathe until each end is the size of the coin to be struck, exactly fitting into the

Steam Coining Press, about 1870

ring made for it. On the smooth surface of each end the die-
cutter engraves the design intended to be in raised letters and
figures on the coin.

When numerous copies of a die are required, as in a national
mint, the first die cut is called the master die. This is cut in soft
steel, which is hardened by heating and then cooling in water. An
impression of this master die is taken in soft steel, which in turn is
hardened. This latter makes a punch which can produce as many
dies as required. (In the early days only the original engravings
were used, and this accounts for the discrepancies you can detect
on old coins: the dies soon wore out and new dies had to be
engraved by hand.)

In the United States, for instance, the process now employed
in making dies is to prepare a model of the coin several times
larger than the finished coin is to be. From this an electrotype is

made, and the dies are cut by a machine called the pantographic die-cutter.

The presses work automatically, except that the planchets are fed by hand into the vertical tubes. They are seized one at a time by automatic fingers, and each one is centered between the two discs. The dies are brought together by the operation of a toggle joint with a pressure varying from 175 tons for a dollar, 119 tons for a half-dollar, 80 tons for a quarter, to 40 tons for a dime. This impact stamps the metal on both sides and forces the planchet to spread out and fill the tube, which is grooved on the inside for reeding the edge of the coin. The large coins are stamped at the rate of 80 to 90 a minute, while the smaller ones are struck at 120 a minute.

It is now the law in the United States and in some other countries that at the end of each year all dies must be destroyed and new ones put into operation.

Further details on this interesting subject can be found in E. O. Webb's book, *Our Metallic Money*, which was published in 1936.

CHAPTER 3

Counterfeiting,

The Oldest Profession

The history of coinage involves the history of counterfeiting as well, because from the time of the first mint men have always known how to copy coins for the purpose of illegal gain. It is still common for a collector to find ancient coins which are obviously counterfeits. For example, not uncommon are forged specimens of the rude coins of Aegina and Lydia.

Herodotus, the "father of history," who lived about five hundred years before the Christian era, wrote that it was rumored: "Polycrates struck off a large number of pieces of lead cased with gold like the coin of the country" and with these paid the Lacedaemonian soldiers who had refused to disperse without their wages. Even if this account is not strictly true, at least it proves that counterfeit money was a matter of common talk and that people knew it could be made well enough to deceive the army of Lacedaemonians.

It was usual for crafty criminals to counterfeit the money of the ancient cities which were renowned for their luxurious ways— cities like Tarentum, Metapontum, and Thurium, where the proverbial Sybarites lived—because money was so carelessly spent in those places that people did not pause to study the coins. It is not surprising that the luxury and vice of those celebrated cities led to crime, for the forging of money may have seemed necessary to furnish the means for the idle to put on a very elaborate front, giving expensive dinner parties and travelling about in style.

However, we read that "those cities distinguished for their strict manners, like Athens and Thebes," had very few counterfeiters. And very few false coins have been found from the reign of Alexander the Great, perhaps because of his good administration.

About 400 B.C. a monetary convention was held by the financiers of the city of Phocaea in Ionia and the city of Mytilene in Lesbos. It was resolved that both cities should issue the same quantities of coins of the same standard, to be made of electrum. Since this alloy could be duplicated and was therefore a temptation to dishonesty, the convention passed another resolution decreeing the death penalty for any officer found guilty of debasing the quality of the metal.

In all ages offenses against the standard coin were punished severely, since they were considered pernicious to the State and a direct interference with the prerogative of the sovereign. Today counterfeiting is punished more humanely than formerly—except in China, where, until recently, beheading was the reward of the counterfeiter. In most countries a long term of imprisonment is the usual sentence.

Among the Romans, false coiners and those who harbored them were alike open to arrest by any person, and the accuser was always amply rewarded: that is, a free person was exempted from taxes for life, and a slave was given his freedom. The forger and also anyone allowing the forger to escape were executed; if he happened to be a freeman he was thrown into the arena with starving beasts, if a slave he was hanged.

The rapacity, luxury and prodigality of the Roman emperors, combined with their immense military establishments, must frequently have involved them in great financial difficulties. It is known that they often coined large amounts of money without protecting its value, in the same way that Henry VIII did many years later in England.

Constantine the Great adjudged false coiners guilty of high treason and condemned them to be burnt alive. Nevertheless, the crime increased, especially among those who considered themselves exempt from punishment. Constantine finally had to ordain that even magistrates found guilty of false coining would be banished. Since that law too failed to check the evil, two years later he decreed that any person of any class whatever, if found guilty of counterfeiting, would be executed.

After the fall of the Roman Empire, the coins of the Middle Ages were very thin, probably because there were no longer such skilled metallurgists. Of course this thinness invited the crime of "clipping" by unscrupulous persons who made good use of the slivers of metal they pared off the edges of coins with shears. In an effort to protect the coins from this theft, many governments passed laws threatening clippers with severe penalties. Only during the Machine Age did this usage abate, when the method of milling the edges of coins was introduced.

Certainly in the Middle Ages even cruel punishment for offenders failed to halt the practice. In the year 1123 the crime had so greatly increased that forgers and those who circulated base coin were declared by the Council of Lateran to be "accursed, oppressors of the poor, disturbers of the State," and were excommunicated. At another time His Holiness John XXII made a grand procession for the purpose of excommunicating all those who had struck florins of an inferior standard. The guilty were sometimes bound two by two and carried in carts to the king's court, where they were sentenced to be mutilated and fined.

In the time of the Anglo-Saxons, the laws of Athelstane declared that a counterfeiter would lose the hand with which he had committed the crime, but later it was decreed that "a man accused of false coining shall go to the three-fold ordeal and if found guilty shall suffer death." The "ordeal" included the placing of the hand in fire without wincing and it was considered that only an innocent person could draw enough heavenly assistance to withstand such suffering. One statute reads that "moneyers who illegally work in a wood, or elsewhere, shall forfeit their lives unless pardoned by the king." This was probably the time when the term "bush-mint" first came into use. The laws of Canute doomed the forger to lose both hands "which are not to be ransomed either with gold or silver."

Under the Norman rule, forgery increased to such an extent that Henry I convened the Grand Council at London in 1105 and caused a law to be passed to the effect that a forger would not only lose his hand but would also be deprived of his sight and subjected to other mutilations.

During the reign of Edward III the "counterfeiting of the king's coin or the bringing into the realm of counterfeit money to the likeness of the authorized currency" was declared treason, and a guilty man was "drawn and quartered and hanged till dead." A guilty woman was burned to death. One exception was reported for an abbot found guilty: being a person of such high degree, he was drawn and hanged, but not quartered.

In 1125 English coins had become so corrupt that a large proportion of them were refused by the merchants, and in 1204 King John proclaimed that coins clipped more than one eighth of their original size were no longer legal tender. He fixed the rate for exchanging "fine and pure silver at the king's exchanges of England and at the archbishop's exchange of Canterbury at sixpense in the pound."

In 1318 there was so much false money in circulation that the barons of the exchequer ordered that "no man should import into the realm clipt money or foreign counterfeit money, under great penalites, and that such persons as had any clipt money in their hands should bore it through in the middle, and bring it to the king's cambium to be recoined." Jurors were required by their oath to report to the king all clippings and coining that came to their knowledge.

One record of the thirty-seventh year of the reign of Henry VIII (1546) states: "This yere, in Februarie, should a woman haue been brent in Smithfield for clipping of gold, but the kynge's pardon came, she beying at the stake ready to be brente." In 1561 a mill was introduced in the English mint by one Eloye Mastrel. Stephen Martin Leakes, in *An Historical Account of English Money*, published in 1793, wrote: "But this Frenchman being detected of counterfeiting and making milled money of the mint, he was hanged and quartered."

In the same century there was a scarcity of money in Germany and an organized band of forgers resided in France in order to be safe from arrest. Many French nobles retained these professional forgers in their castles, dignified them with the title of "philosophers," and treated them like honored guests, even "admitting them to their tables." Because they refrained from counterfeiting French coins and confined their attentions to ducats, thalers, and florins, they deemed themselves above reproach. Charles XI, who reigned from 1560 to 1574, was himself an expert counterfeiter, and he devoted much of his leisure time to this pursuit.

In Padua, Italy, about 1540, Jean Cavino and Alexander Bassiano, became famous as manufacturers of copies of coins and medals. Three of the most celebrated counterfeiters were Dervien, in Italy, Carteron in Holland, and Congornier in France. In 1826 Sestini published a catalog of the forged coins of Becker, who died at Hamburg four years after the date of that publication.

It may seem incredible that a counterfeit coin could ever be of higher intrinsic value than the genuine, and yet this singular instance did occur within the last century. The Government of Haiti coined base metal for money but regulated the importation of silver so that the value of the coin would not be affected. Nevertheless, pure silver coins of the same weight and size were manufactured in New York, smuggled into Haiti, and there passed for genuine coin.

A modern counterfeit is represented by the many copies of the 8 annas of India, which was coined only in 1919. While the genuine one is not rare, it is difficult to obtain. The natives, long practiced in the art of faking, were quick to discover an easy method of imitating it. The hardness of the alloy made it possible for them to press it into a piece of red-hot iron and produce a die for striking counterfeits in a softer metal. The coinage was therefore discontinued.

In some show places of the Near East, tourist guides have been known to bury spurious coins ahead of time and then "accidentally" excavate them before the eyes of tourists—who readily bought the coins at high prices.

In his essay on *Medals,* published in 1789, John Pinkerton declared that a collector of coins ought first to study the coins themselves, before referring to books. He called attention to the fact that a student can distinguish a certain book from a thousand others, that a shepherd knows his own rams and ewes—and that it is easy for a trained collector to say, "This is a false coin, and this is a genuine one."

CHAPTER 4

Ancient and Medieval Coins

When we study history it is important for us to see each country
and its topography and its relation to other countries, as well as to
know the character of the people by means of their heroes. There
would be no good in any knowledge of the past unless we could
see it as a reality in relation to the present. Coins are records for
interpreting, visualizing, and vitalizing ancient history. They
inform us of events and the good and evil deeds of people, and the
fluctuation of governments during the vast period covered by
coinage.

Although narrative history tells us very little about ancient
coinage, we are able to piece together enough details to make
quite a story. Money is often referred to in the Old Testament, but
there was no coined money in the most magnificent civilizations
ever known—neither in Babylonia (out of which came Abraham
and his descendants) nor in Egypt (out of which the children of
Israel moved to Canaan). In the time of Alexander the Great (336
B.C.) several cities near Jerusalem, such as Tyre, Sidon and Joppa,
had mints of their own. Even before that, Greek Imperial coins
were minted in the various cities of Greece, as well as later when
they were under the dominion of the Romans.

In *Maccabaeans 15:6* we read that in the year 139 B.C. Simon
Maccabaeus, the high priest in Jerusalem, issued the first Hebrew
coinage. He coined silver shekels and also half-shekels, inscribing
them according to their weight.

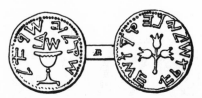

Shekel (Silver), 135 B.C., worth $110

The Bible mention of the widow's mite is of special interest, and we know that the mites of Pilate and Tiberius were in circulation when Jesus walked the streets of Jerusalem. One type bore the picture of a cup, or the ladle used in the Temple. On the Reverse the inscription was "Julia the Mother of Caesar."

Probably no passage in the Bible excites greater interest than the account of Judas' betrayal of Jesus for "thirty pieces of silver." Those pieces were either Roman denarii or Greek tetradrachms. The denarius ("piece of ten units") was a silver coin a trifle lighter than the Attic drachm, and it appeared about 300 years earlier. It is more likely that Judas' payment was in tetradrachms, since the denarii were of far less value, and it is said that the sum of money he received was "sufficient to buy a piece of land near the city."

GREEK AND ROMAN COINS

From the standpoint of mythology, history, and art, the coins of ancient Greece are absolutely unrivaled. Artistically many of them excel all modern coins in purity of their lines, bold relief, and delicacy of treatment. Many people regard a fine Greek coin as the most convenient, most compact, best preserved, and most beautiful relic of antiquity.

(Bronze), about 285 B.C., worth $4

The study of the coinage of ancient Greece offers such a vast field for research, and the material is so abundant and varied, that a collector is always challenged by the magnitude of the subject. The religion and politics of those old cities, their rise and fall, the legends of their heroes, and the gradual growth of art can all be studied from the workmanship on their coins.

The most important cities of the ancient world were Athens, Thebes, Corinth, Aegina, and those that belonged to the Achaean and Lycian Leagues. Among the cults illustrated by coins are those of Zeus, Apollo, Aphrodite, Pallas Athene, and the demi-god Heracles. Some of the most famous works of art are on coins: the Olympian Zeus, the statue of Athene by Phidias, and the olive-wood figure of Athene. Among the religious symbols are the Corinthian swastika, the Aecid shield of Thebes, the tortoise of Aphrodite, and Apollo's lyre. They revive for us the folk-tales of the days of Homer and Hesiod.

Although there are many collectors of Roman coins, there are few people patient enough to specialize in collecting the ancient Greek coins. This is regrettable, for it was from the Greeks that the Romans learned not only architecture and sculpture but also the art of engraving gems and coin-dies.

Any student of the history of art must begin with the study of Greek coinage. A little coin preserves the sublime thoughts of poets and philosophers and also the brave struggles against evil and ignorance. The coins of many cities, such as Syracuse and Tarentum, were designed and executed by great artists, and in all the ages they have been treasured as gems. Many a page of Homer and Pindar, of Herodotus and Thucydides, of Polybius and Plutarch, will be opened to a collector of Greek coins as a result of the questions raised by the ancient engravings.

Of course everything that awakens an echo of the glory of Athens is imbued with her charm, and no one can regard the owl-stamped coins without associating them with men whom we must regard as the world's greatest thinkers. Owls were always numerous among the rocky hills of Athens, and they are still common there. What the doves were to Sicyon, the eagles to Elis, the wild swans to Clazomene, the owls were to Athens—objects which reminded the citizen of his home wherever they were seen. (So in our time doves are associated with Venice and storks with Nuremberg.) The owl is a bird of the night, and it may be for that reason that on the Reverse of the tetradrachms, in the days of Hippias, the crescent moon was shown behind the figure of the owl.

The Corinthian colts were earlier than the Athenian owls, but the tortoises of Aegina were on the earliest of all Greek coins. Tortoises were common on the shores of Aegina and they were chosen as the symbol for the first coins struck in the temple of Aphrodite Urania of Aegina. They were the emblem of Aphrodite, the goddess born of the sea foams in which the tortoises were found. Plutarch tells the story of Theseus who threw the robber Sciron over the cliff to be devoured by a giant sea-tortoise, thus causing him to suffer the fate he had inflicted upon others.

For sixty or seventy years the tortoise coinage of Aegina was used by the Corinthian merchants. The Corinthians had derived their standard for weighing gold and silver from Asia Minor, their unit of weight being the Babylonian stater of 130 grams.

They also adopted the Eastern system of dividing by three and six. This way of dividing passed on to the Corinthian colonies in the West, as can be seen from the weights of the coins of Croton, Sybaris and Metapontum. The coiners of these cities also copied the flat fabric of the Corinthians and the incuse Reverse type (having the hollow indent of the Obverse design).

Although the winged-horse coins were common to about twenty cities, there is no reason to suppose that the use of this type implied any treaties between Corinth and the other towns. The choice was probably made independently by each city on account of its being readily accepted. People may have taken it for granted that all money should have this symbol.

The Pegasus on the Obverse of the Corinthian coinage is connected with many myths which, although different in place and date of origin, became welded together to form the well-known legend of the Corinthian hero Bellerophon. It is perhaps impossible to determine what the symbol of the winged horse meant to the citizens of the days of Periander. The earliest poet to write on the subject was the author of the *Theogonia* (a Boeotian poet who was a follower of Hesiod) about a hundred years before the coins were designed, and even then the legend was confused with that of Perseus. About one hundred and sixty years after the first issue of these coins, Pindar completed the fusion of the myths. It seems probable that the seafaring merchants of Corinth in the days of Periander chose the symbol of Pegasus as an emblem of Poseidon, rather than as the expression of the complicated ideas of the learned author of *Theogonia*.

The rose on the coins of Rhodes was probably chosen because that flower was the emblem of their sun-god, Helios. The head of Helios is on the Obverse.

The lyre on coins of Colophon does not signify a trade in musical instruments—it is the symbol of Apollo.

There is a myth concerning the decision of the Athenians as to which deity they would worship. Servius, in his notes on Virgil (*Georgias*, I, 12), and Herodotus (VIII, 55) both record that Poseidon and Pallas Athene were contending for the honor of sponsoring the rising city. It was agreed that the one who gave the best gift to the people should rule them. Poseidon struck the shore with his trident and produced a horse, the symbol of war. Athene cast her spear and brought forth an olive tree. Since the olive tree was a symbol of peace, the people preferred it, and therefore they built their temples in honor of Pallas Athene.

As Athens developed in power and wealth, her sculpture and architecture developed also. From the days of Phidias to those of Plato, the worldly wisdom and prudence, the technical skill of artists and craftsmen, and the strategy of generals—all the powers of which the Athenians were proud—were attributed to the Parthenon, where their goddess reigned to guide them.

Greek coin types are of two classes: (1) mythological and religious representations, and (2) portraits of historical personages. The period when human heads first appeared upon coins was about 400 B.C., and ever since then the coins of all the nations of the world have been faithful historians. We are indebted to coins alone for prized portraits of the most noted characters in history.

Coin engraving is the offspring of the art of sculpture. Not only is a record of lost statues preserved to us in the design of ancient coins, but the coins of Greece afford admirable examples of that skill by which her sculptors obtained their renown. The period of finest Greek art, as shown by Greek coins, was from 415 B.C. (when the Athenians made their expedition against Sicily) to 335 B.C. (when Alexander the Great made his great conquest). The excellence of the coins is so great that, were it not for their smallness, they would be used as the finest art studies in the world. They tell us what other monuments leave untold, filling up gaps in our knowledge of antiquity and revealing things that are known from them alone. Even the common coins vividly illuminate dark spaces in the world's history, and artistically many of them are far superior to our modern coins.

On the coins struck during the early part of the reign of Alexander the Great, the head represents Heracles, the national hero who was regarded as the son of Zeus. Some collectors think that a portrait of Alexander himself, wearing a lion's skin, is on some of his later coins. The head is an example of refined manly beauty, the nose slightly curved, the upper lip short, the lips full and the brow prominent, the face clean-shaven and the hair in short locks.

Roman coins, though they can never compare with Greek coins as works of art, worthily represent the Graeco-Roman art of the Empire, and some of them present portraits of remarkable beauty. In fact, they are a vast gazette proclaiming customs, faiths, wealth, culture, victories, and down-falls.

The large bronze pound or as (now worth $40) was the unit of coinage before the City of Seven Hills had become a world power using a more valuable metal as medium of exchange, with coins of various denominations. The oldest Roman coin extant, a gigantic piece of copper weighing less than five pounds, probably dates from 600 to 500 B.C. It too was called the aes or as, and it was subsequently changed in size and form, but it remained a Roman coin down to modern times. This money of Rome was held as a reserve, and it was represented in circulation by leather notes.

The as was used by the boys of Rome as coppers are now used, for winning arguments or selecting a leader. But instead of crying, "Heads or tails!" they cried, "Heads or ship!"—"*Capita aut Navem!*"—alluding to the heads of Janus and the prow of a ship on the opposite sides of the coin. This expression, "*Capita aut Navem,*" continued in use among the Romans centuries after the heads of Janus and the ship's prow were no longer shown on the coinage.

The Romans had learned from the Greeks the advantages of money issued by the State only, with no worth but that which it derived from its usefulness and efficiency in measuring the value of commodities and services. In order to maintain such a money the State monopolized the copper mines, restricted commerce in copper, struck copper pieces of high artistic merit in order to make counterfeiting difficult, and stamped them with the mark of the State. These pieces were then declared the sole legal tender for the payment of domestic contracts, taxes, fines, and debts. Their issue was limited until universal demand and their comparative scarcity raised their value above that of the metal of which they were composed. For foreign trade or diplomacy the Romans kept a supply of gold and silver, coined or uncoined.

Contrary to what we might expect, many ancient Greek and Roman coins over 1800 years old and entirely genuine are not rare. This is because great quantities were struck. Easily available, at about 50¢ apiece, are good specimens of Roman bronze coins bearing the portraits of some of the first twelve Caesars. Greek and Roman copper coins in fair condition can be bought today for as little as $20 for 100. There are of course some rarities, but compared to the bulk these are few in number.

The rare ones are of high value if they can be found in a good state of preservation. Prices for nearly all classes of ancient coins fluctuate; while one type may be moderately priced today, it may bound upward in price within a year. For this reason no reliable table of premiums on Greek and Roman coins can yet be given, although in these pages you will find the prices listed for the commoner Roman bronze coins, and other useful information.

Here are some examples of the Roman dinarius or silver coin:

Pompey the Great, 48 B.C., worth $8

Galba, 68–69 A.D.,
worth $3

Trajan, 98–117 A.D.,
worth $1.50

And here are some types of ancient Greek coins:

Corinth, 400–338 B.C., worth $7

Tetradrachm of Athéns, about 350 B.C., worth $12

Gold Stater of Alexander, about 300 B.C., worth $40

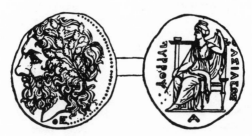

Pyrrhus, 275 B.C., worth $20

As previously stated, the coining of money always symbolized sovereignty. Since the supremacy of Rome was so widely accepted, for centuries neither the subject provinces nor the so-called independent states adjacent ever attempted to coin gold money. If we assume that the Christian princes were really independent sovereigns before the destruction of the Roman Empire by the fall of Constantinople in 1204, how can we explain that none of them ever struck a gold coin before that event, and all of them struck gold coins immediately afterward?

In cities where silver was sufficiently abundant, copper was not readily accepted by the people, because the value of copper was so low that only a large piece could represent enough of a value (as at Rome, where the aes grave was very heavy). The Athenians had very small fractions of drachms struck in silver, and therefore they did not need smaller denominations in copper. People in those days also had a custom of carrying small change in the mouth, and naturally copper coins were unpleasant-tasting and unwholesome.

The men who founded the commerce and colonies of Corinth must have been more than ordinarily courageous to brave the perils of the ocean, the only known region then unclaimed by any earthly ruler. Every land was under the sway of some king or tyrant who tried to defend his flock, but those who ventured on the seas were obliged to look to their own defense, and there were many pirates abroad.

The earliest of the Corinthian Tyrants was Cypselus, who began to rule in 655 B.C., and it was his son, Periander, who introduced the first coinage in Corinth.

ITALIAN COINS

After the Roman Empire had fallen, the art of coinage in what we now know as Italy was lost. After the extinction of the Gothic kings, coins of the ex-archs of Ravenna appeared, since they were viceroys of the emperors of the East. These coins were only small coppers, and they usually bore the inscription *Felix Ravenna.*

The first coins of the modern series are those issued by Charlemagne at Milan about 780 A.D. They bear a cross, and on the Reverse there is the monogram of Carolus. These Milanese coins were issued by successive German emperors up to the thirteenth century.

After the period of Charlemagne the modern coinage of silver pennies commenced. They, like those of France and Spain and England, were modeled on the old Roman denarius.

The modern coinage of the city of Rome under the Popes began with the silver pennies of Pope Hadrian, from 771 to 795 A.D. This series has the name of the Pope on one side and SCVS PETRVS on the other. A few of them have rude portraits, such as those of Benedict II, Sergius III, John X, or Agapetus II.

In Milan the remarkable coins of the Visconti, the independent dukes of Milan, began with those of Azio in 1330. Ludovic il Mauro had on his coinage the legend LVDOVICVS *M*SF *ANGLVS*DVX*MLI**. The meaning of ANGLVS has not yet been satisfactorily explained.

Florence is credited as the first community to introduce the general use of gold in coinage. It was probably the Florentine bankers who prompted the revival of gold coinage for their business convenience, and the beautiful fionino d'oro was issued about 1252 (a century earlier than the famous issue of gold nobles in England). These gold pieces bore on one side the Florentine lily for principal type, and on the other a figure of St. John the Baptist, the patron saint of the city. They were later imitated by the French and the Popes, then by the Germans and the English.

In 1194 Naples and Sicily were subdued by the German emperors, whose Neapolitan coins are extant. The coins of Manfred appeared in 1225, those of Charles of Provence in 1266, followed by those of Queen Jeanne and those of the House of Aragon. The later series began to show improvement toward the close of the 15th century. Soon afterward the Italian coinage assumed a strong resemblance to that of the rest of modern Europe.

NORSE MONEY

The evolution of Norse monetary systems, whether in Iestia, Saxony, Scandinavia, Frankland, Britain, Russia, or Iceland, usually showed this trend: (1) fish and vadmal (cloth money); (2)baug or ring money; (3) imitations of pagan-Roman coined money; (4) Norse pagan pieces partly derived from the Roman: stycas, scats, and oras; (5) instrusions of Moslem dinars, maravedis and dirhems; (6) replacement of the last by Christian-Roman pounds, shillings, and pence. These changes of course did not occur simultaneously in the various countries (the Goths, for instance, were using coined money in Britain before they employed fish money in Iceland), but it was the usual order of progress in each country or petty kingdom by itself. From the period of their original settlement in Britain down to their contact with the Brigantes, the Norsemen used no coined money at all. Indeed, they had little or no commerce, for they lived chiefly by hunting, fishing, and plundering.

The earliest coins imputed to the kings of Sweden are the silver pieces of Biorn, 818 A.D., and they were imitations of those of Charlemagne, even having the cross stamped upon them, although Biorn was not a Christian.

Denmark, Sweden, and Norway all developed their coinage systems in a way that resembles the progress of the English monarchy. On the coins of Hacon (1067) the name reads AACVNE. The series can be traced to 1387, when Margaret, Queen of Sweden and Denmark, was portrayed on a coin. But the designs were quite crude.

The first coins known to have come from Norway were those of Olaf in 1026, and they bear the legend OLAF REX NOR. Some Norwegian coins have on the Reverse the letters NI. for NIDAROS, NODROSEN, or NIDSEN, now Drontheim, the capital.

Below are illustrations of some crowns and thalers from Saxony. Coins of this type usually retail for from $6 to $20. Of course there are rarities which are worth considerably more.

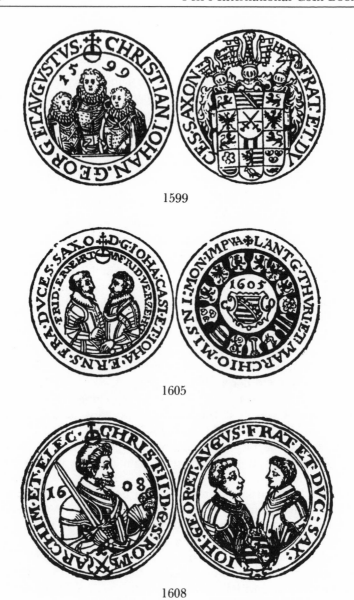

1599

1605

1608

Undated, about 1600

1623

1624

BRITISH COINS

The word shilling for the English coin has been said by some to be derived from the Latin *sicilicus* (quarter ounce) and by others to have come from a Saxon word signifying a scale. The pound was, of course, originally a weight, but the standard English gold pound was always about the value of the ancient Greek stater.

The coinage of Scotland does not go back to a very remote period and extends only from David I (1124) to Anne (1711). The earliest Scottish coins are said to be those of Alexander I (1107), but other authorities claim that no coinage at all can be assigned to Alexander I. The thistle first appeared on gold and silver coins during the reign of James V.

Irish gun money has evoked a pathetic interest unequalled by any other series. Its issue in 1689 and the misery which it wrought made such an impression upon the Irish people that it has remained in the popular memory. King James II had fled to the protection of his Irish subjects, and as far as the English were concerned he was an outlaw. All the gun money, except the crown, was dated with a month as well as the year of issue. Collectors have found half-crowns, shillings and sixpence for January, February, and March, 1689. However, the issue of this gun money was decreed by royal edict of June 18, 1689, and that edict relates only to the sixpence. In fact, the sixpence is the only one of the series which bears the June date, and there are no pieces at all of any denomination for April and May of that year, while for July all three denominations of 1689 are available. It is pretty well established that the coins marked for the first three months were antedated.

The proclamation of James II concerning the gun money contains this interesting passage:

> Wheras we are informed that several covetous persons, who have a greater regard for their own private interest than for the public good, have been giving of late intolerable rates for gold and silver. . . .

It was forbidden on pain of death to give more than thirty shillings in brass or copper money for a French Louis d'Or, or more than seven shillings brass for a silver dollar.

In February, 1690, King William issued a counter-proclamation declaring the gun money illegal and of no value whatsoever. This plunged the Irish people into a depression.

Large hoards of gun money are continually being uncovered in Ireland. It is said that those who bartered everything they possessed for it, on the strength of their faith in James II, were so ashamed of their folly that they preferred to hide it rather than put it into circulation as pence, halfpence and farthings. Some say that the English word "humbug" is but a distortion of the Gaelic "ulmbog" (soft copper), an Irish-peasant term of contempt which they applied to gun money.

FRENCH COINS

The French are credited with having made the greatest improvements in modern coinage. Their coins are a history of their nation, beginning with the small coin issued in the reign of Louis the Meek and continuing to the last currency of the Republic of France, spanning a period of one thousand years.

LORRAINE COINS

The first hereditary power of the House of Lorraine endured for seven centuries, during which time a series of money little inferior to that of the great European monarchies was issued.

The transition from the medieval to the modern style of art took place during the long reign of Charles III, which began in 1545.

PRUSSIAN COINS

The first Prussian silver pennies were coined by the Teutonic
Order at Culm in the 12th century. Later the rulers of Prussia
coined schillings, groats, and schots, the last being the largest and
consequently the most rare in collections.

After Charlemagne, Germany consisted of an immense number of small independent states, to each of which the emperor,
Henry the Falconer, gave the privilege of coining money, from
about the year 920 A.D. Augsburg, Hamburg, Frankfurt, Stras-
bourg, and many others were true republics in the heart of the
empire. To give a description of all these issues would be an
endless task.

HUNGARIAN COINS

Bohemia, the most westerly and purely Slavonic state, had the
earliest coinage. It began with that of Duke Boleslaus in 909 A.D.,
and the coins bore both his portrait and his name.

The coinage of Hungary belongs to a similar class as that of
Bohemia. The Bracteate money of Ottocar (1197 A.D.) was like
that issued about the same time in several parts of Europe. It was
made of very thin silver impressed on only one side, the Reverse
having the hollow indent of the same form (incuse type).

The coinage of Poland followed a similar course in its development.

MEXICAN COINS

The Mexicans used only gold and silver, and their national series
is full of tragic interest since it embraces three and a half centuries
of Mexican history, from Cortez (1547) to Maximilian (1867). The
pillar dollar, the windmill dollar, the cob money, and the cast
dollar are good collector's items.

8 Reales (Copper), 1813, worth $4

Additional basis for the speculation that the Aztecs originated in Asia is shown on the Revolutionary coin illustrated above. The bow and arrow symbol on this is *exactly* like the design which appears on certain thick native money of Indian called dumps.

SPANISH AND PORTUGUESE COINS

Until the irruption of the Moors in 714 A.D., Spain formed one compact and powerful kingdom. Their princes had received the privilege of coining from the early emperors of the East. They issued a gold coinage of great interest—trientes, or thirds of the Byzantine solidus, which, under the name of bezants, long circulated in the west and north of Europe.

The Gothic inhabitants of Spain, driven into the fastnesses of the Austrian mountains, step by step recovered their territories from the Oriental invaders. In the tenth century, when the kingdoms of Aragon and Navarre were founded, their coins closely resembled the silver pennies of the rest of Europe. The kingdom of Castile was next founded, and the Moors were finally expelled from their last stronghold, Granada. The whole Iberian Peninsula in 1492 fell under the reign of Ferdinand and Isabella. They were heirs of the kingdom of Castille and Aragon, which had previously absorbed all the lesser states.

The coinage of Portugal and Spain in the fifteenth century held greater sway than that of other countries of the time. The joe and half-joe of Portugal were widely known, while the Spanish dollar, with its pretentious two globes under a crown, was a symbol of the limitless rule of the great Philip. The coins of these two nations, because of their possessions in the New World, became the circulating medium of that portion of the earth. Spanish and Mexican dollars were almost synonymous, while the real and the joe of South America were patterned after those of Portugal.

NETHERLANDS COINS

The coinage of the countries of Holland and Flanders followed much the same course as that of Bar or Lorraine.

Origin of the Dollar: In the year 1300, Count von Schlick, commanding a force of mounted free lances, captured the St. Joachims Thal (valley) in Bohemia, with its silver mines. He mined the silver but the natives refused to accept the ingots in exchange for their products. In order to buy provisions for his soldiers, von Schlick coined a silver disc showing the picture of St. Joachim with a view of the Thal, and on the Reverse a Bohemian lion rampant. He named the disc St. Joachim's thaler. The natives were pleased with this and readily sold their products in exchange for thalers. The shrewd Dutch envoy sent a sample of the money to Holland, where a similar disc was minted and named a dolar. The English not long afterward minted a disc of their own and named it the dollar.

RUSSIAN COINS

In 981 A.D., when Vladimir, or Volodemir I, Duke of Russia, married the daughter of the Byzantine emperor, art first dawned in this country. The Tartar conquest of 1238 interrupted the course of civilization, and not until 1462, when the foreign yoke was thrown off, did the modern sovereigns appear. The earliest coins usually have a man standing with a bow, or a spear, for principal type, somewhat similar to the coins of the Scythian dynasties that subdued the north of India. On the Reverse there are rude figures of different animals.

Under Ivan, or John, in 1547, the Russian dollar or rouble appeared, as well as the half-rouble.

CHINESE COINS

Of the several thousand known coins of the Celestial Empire, most of them are bronzed. They depict the way dynasty succeeded dynasty, and the way usurpation was followed by insurrection. The Chinese claim to have had an uninterrupted coinage for forty-nine centuries.

Large numbers of their coins, covered with cabalistic characters or symbolic animals, have at times been considered charms to protect against fever or supernatural menace. The ancient Chinese had a reverence for the coin-charm, and a small coin was often placed in the mouth of the dead. Even not long ago in California, if a Chinese died, some member of his family placed a small silver coin on his tongue as a blessing.

CHAPTER 5

Strange Money

Only a few metals have missed serving at some time or another as material for coinage. Iron was used in the fifth century B.C. and again in Poland and Germany from 1916 to 1918; zinc in Czechoslovakia; lead in Egypt before the Christian era and in Denmark as late as the seventeenth century. Of course gold and silver and copper have always been widely used. Tin halfpennies and farthings were current coin in England prior to 1692. Platinum was struck in Russia a century ago. Nickel, now so popular on the continent of Europe, was in circulation under some of the kings of Bactria soon after 200 B.C. Brass, electrum, billon, potin, and aluminum are some other metals that have been used for money.

But not only metals have served as a medium of exchange. Here is a partial list of other commodities that have taken part in commercial transactions:

Tobacco (Virginia colonies)
Wampum (Massachusetts colonies as well as among Indian tribes)
Cocoa seed (Aztecs)
Seed pod (Peru)
Fish (Saxony and Scandinavia)
Cowrie shells (Timbuktu)
Rings and bracelets (Nile Valley)
Iron knives (China)
Arrowheads (American Indians)
Musket balls (Massachusetts colonies)
Cotton cloth (Africa)
Glass beads (Abyssinia)

Salt (Abyssinia)
Linen cloth (Saxony and Scandinavia)
Cattle (Saxony and Scandinavia)
Fish hooks (Ceylon)
Gold dust (Senegal and California)
Amber, camels, slaves, incense (Africa)

In modern times, as in Germany during the inflationary period of the early 1920's, currency was printed on silk, leather, and wood.

Ring Money of Sierra Leone, 19th Century, worth $10

Ring money was also used by the ancient Britons before the Roman invasion. These rings are sometimes found today in various parts of England and Ireland, and they are of a fixed weight, proving they were passed as coins. Caesar relates that rings of fixed weight were used for money in Britain and Gaul during his time. Similar reports have come from north Europe.

Fish-hook Money of Ceylon, 19th Century, worth $5

Knife Money of China, 300–200 B.C., worth $3 to $10

STRANGE MONEY OF THE CHINESE

Anyone travelling in the Orient is at first surprised to find a poor woman wearing heavy gold bracelets and anklets. But the surprise disappears when he learns that there is no investment opportunity for money and, as a consequence, the poor and the rich, when they accumulate gold, call in a travelling tinker. He, with his crucible, furnace, and hammer, sits down in the court of the palace or on the dirt floor of the hut and, out of the metal handed him, he fashions a rude bracelet or anklet. This adorns the dusky leg or arm of the favorite wife, until necessity compels its transfer. There is no delay or confusion in the transfer, either. The owner goes into the street to make a purchase and tenders his bracelet in payment. The convenient moneychanger is at hand in every street with his scales. The weight is told, and the merchant accepts the metal object as readily as we would accept coin today.

The Chinese are the only people who have ever made porcelain legal tender. In the early days they, like the Africans, used small seashells in trade. At the time of the earliest records (2300 B.C.) they had learned to use such metals as gold, silver, copper, and tin, yet there was no coinage. All commodities, including wrought and unwrought metal, were bought by weight.

Bronze was not known until about 1741 B.C., when it was brought from Asia Minor by means of caravans. Currency then began to take a definite form and a practical one. Hoes, spades, sickles, and pieces of silk became the mediums of exchange, with tortoise shells and cowries used for smaller denominations. The words tsien and pu, meaning hoes and cloth, grew to be the terms for wealth. About 950 B.C. uninscribed bronze rings were accepted as payment, even for the remission of corporal penalties. During the wars after 679 B.C., the Prince authorized metal knives to be accepted in payment of fines for slight offenses, and thus another step was taken toward an acknowledged currency.

This may have been the origin of inscribed coinage. Sea-traders from the Indian Ocean established a colony in what is now Shantung, and they inscribed an emblem on large bronze knives for currency. The shape was rude and had not yet assumed the symbolical form with the ring at the end.

The earliest forms of this cash, or knife money, bore the place name only, but when the colony became associated with surrounding districts, the knives were marked with the names of the various places where they would be accepted. Later the inscription was simplified to a mere statement of value and name of place where issued. During the seven centuries that preceded the Christian era, these knives were the chief form of currency, although spade money, spread-out money (sometimes called bell cash), and an ancient form of round cash took form gradually from the use of bronze rings and the looped handles of the knives.

It is sometimes said that the use of metallic money in China began in 2746 B.C., when copper coins were cast in the shape of a small sword. Sword money was issued as late as 22 A.D. The oldest round money without inscription was issued about 1121 B.C., while the first inscribed money appeared in 617 B.C. The name of a Chinese ruler was never used on money during his lifetime, his true name coming into use only after his death. The value of copper was set at one hundredth part of the same weight in silver.

STRANGE MONEY OF THE AFRICANS

The primitive peoples of Africa, before the white man entered that continent, had no native coinage, but long before 1872 Spanish and Austrian coins were current in the interior. The natives looked with suspicion upon clean, bright money, for they were

familiar only with coins which bore the effigy of Maria Theresa
or the Pillars of Hercules.

Gold dust was used, but the minkalli (worth about $2.50, or
3000 cowrie shells) was standard. The cowrie had been imported
from Persia, and it was in circulation in Timbuktu as early as the
eleventh century. Along the coast the shells were strung in
bunches of one hundred or two hundred, but in the interior they
were handled singly.

The natives also used strips of cotton cloth called gabaga (the
Arabs called it tari). Narrow cotton strips called leppi equalled
one pound of copper, or eight cowries, or kungona. Big deals
were made with shirts, four of which were worth a Spanish dollar.
In some places the currency was linen for making shirts, thirty
pieces worth one dollar. One piece of dammour, a coarse cotton
cloth, was big enough to make a shirt for a full-grown man.
Indigo-dyed cotton, kaniki, was used before American goods were
introduced. Products from the cotton mills of Massachusetts were
called merkani, the African corruption of the word "American."

Amber, kohl, incense, rhea, oxen, camels, and slaves also
passed current, and rings of various sizes bought small things,
while beads and salt were used for the large purchases. The natives
who sold slaves to the Portuguese traders (each for a piece of iron
called kantai) beat their gold into solid shells which the traders
called spondylus macutus (perhaps the origin of the slang term
"spondulics"). Thirty parcels, each containing ten or twelve
plates of iron, equalled ten rotolo, or a dollar.

Along the Nile the usual currency was small pieces of iron
wrought into lances, knives, or axes, but cows and grain were
used in important transactions. Glass and wooden beads, also the
kernels of the doumpalm nut, circulated as money.

In Abyssinia cloth and salt constituted the currency. Glass
beads of all kinds and colors, perfect or broken, passed for money
and were called borjooke (grains). Shells sold at ten paras for one
cuba (a wooden measure that could hold 62 cubic inches of rain
water).

In nearly every province salt was valuable as a medium of exchange. It was secured from mines near the Red Sea and was cut into eight-inch-square blocks. Two hundred such blocks were worth one dollar.

At Zanzibar beads were sold by the pound. The cheapest were those of white porcelain and the most expensive were the coral beads. There were four hundred varieties, usually strung on threads of palm fiber.

Brass wires in bracelets about three pounds in weight were called kitindi. Along the Nile tributaries, the price of a slave ten years old was 55 copper rotoli or about $7.50. Where English copper bars from Khartoum or lumps of copper from the Dar-mines were used, small change was made with copper armlets or finger rings.

On the southern edge of the Sahara Desert, as far as the sterile shore of the Red Sea, grain constituted the principal medium of exchange because of its scarcity. In districts where food was plentiful there was no evidence of a grain currency; iron hoes, spades, and axes were used.

CHAPTER 6

How to Identify Coins

The first rule to follow in identifying a coin is to look at it and learn as much as you can from the coin itself. When you are familiar with the questions you wish to have answered about it, then you will find some assistance in the following tables.

Table A gives alphabetically place names and words found on coins and the countries where they originated. *Table B* gives alphabetically monetary units, showing the countries which use such names for their money. *Table C* lists countries alphabetically, showing their typical monetary units. *Table D* gives additional place names with their geographical location and the nationality of the money they have used or are using now. *Table E* provides a list of countries whose coins have inscriptions in lettering which are not familiar to English-speaking people. Many such coins are illustrated in this book or described in the text.

TABLE A

Words on Coins

The following are typical words found on coins and the countries in which they have originated. Compare the words on your coins with the column at the left in order to find the name of the country which issued it. Some coins will indicate the name of the country in plain English. Refer to *Table E* if no English appears on the coin. A designation here marked with an asterisk (*) is not the exact lettering on the coin but merely the English letters it most closely resembles. For example, ΛΕΡΤΑ indicates Greece; the word is pronounced Lepta and the Greek letters are not exactly the same as the English letters shown, but they do at first sight look like our spelling of AEPTA. This method is used here merely to help you in your task of identification.

Apparent Lettering on Coin	Nation of Issue
Aargan	Swiss canton
Aeba*	Bulgaria
Aepta*	Greece
Algerie	Algeria
Alwan State	India
Anhalt	German state
Annapa*	Serbia
Antigua	British West Indies
Amvers	Belgium
Apaxmai*	Greece
Appenzell	Swiss Canton
Arequipa	Peru
Austriae	Austria Hungary
Baden	German state
Bank of Montreal	Canada
Barcelona	Spain
Bayern	German state
Belges	Belgium
Belgie	Belgium
Belgische Cong	Belgian Congo
Bern	Swiss canton
Bikanir State	India
Bogota	Colombia
Bon	Austria Hungary
Boliviana	Bolivia
Bourbon	Isle de Bourbon
Bras	Brazil

Apparent Lettering on Coin	Nation of Issue
Brasil	Brazil
Britan	England
Britannia	England
Britanniarum	England
Buenos Ayres	Argentina
Caracas	Venezuela
CCCP	Soviet Russia
Centro de America	Guatemala, Costa Rica, or Honduras
Colonies Francaises	French colonies
Congo	Belgian Congo
Cordoba	Argentina
CTOTNHKN*	Bulgaria
Cuzco	Peru
Dan	Denmark
Daniae	Denmark
Danmark	Denmark
Dansk-Amerik	Danish West Indies
Deutsches Reich	Germany
Demerary & Essequibo	British Guiana
D'Haiti	Haiti
DNHAPA*	Yugoslavia
D.O.A.	German East Africa
Durango	Mexico
EESTI*	Estonia
Eire	Ireland
Escalin	San Domingo
Espanas	Spain
Etruria	Italy
Filipinas	Philippine Islands
Françoise	France
Fukrin	China
Fung Tien	China

Apparent Lettering on Coin	Nation of Issue
Gaule	Italy
Geneva	Swiss canton
Genuensis	Italy
Gronlands	Greenland
Groszy	Poland
Guyane	French Guiana
Hamburg	Germany
Hamburger	Germany
Helvet	Switzerland
Helvetia	Switzerland
Hessen	German state
Hibernia	Spain
Hisp	Spain
Holl	Netherlands
Hollandia	Netherlands
Hung	Austria Hungary
Hu Peh	China
Hu Pu	China
HAPA*	Serbia
HARA*	Montenegro
HEPIIEPA*	Montenegro
Indo-Chine	Indo-China
In Hoc Signo Vinces	Brazil or Portugal
Ionikon	Greece
Island of Sultana	Labuan, island near North Borneo
Italia	Italy
Jalisco	Mexico
Koll*	Russia
Kuang Ksu	China
La Paz	Bolivia
Latvias	Latvia
Liban	Lebanon

Apparent Lettering on Coin	Nation of Issue
Lietuva	Lithuania
L.V.O.	Mexico
Macuta	Portuguese West Africa
Madeirensis	Portugal
Magdalen Island	Canada
Manks	Great Britain, Isle of Man
Markkaa	Finland
Mexicana	Mexico
M.O.	Mexico
Mocambique	Portuguese East Africa
MOHETA*	Russia
Ned.	Netherlands
Nederlanden	Netherlands
Nederlandischen Indie	Dutch Indies
Neu-Guinea	German New Guinea
Nueva Grenada	Colombia
Norges	Norway
Oesterreich	Austria
Oldenburg	German state
Ostrafrikanische	German East Africa
Osterreich	Austria
Ouest Africain	French West Africa
Pennia	Finland
Polski	Poland
Pon. Max	Papal (Vatican)
Port	Portugal
Portug	Portugal
Portugueza Africa	Portuguese West Africa
Preussen	German state
Prov. de Guiana	Spanish Guiana
Province du Bas	Canada
Porto Rico	Puerto Rico
Pybab*	Russia

Apparent Lettering
on Coin   Nation of Issue

Quebec	Canada
REAL	Curacao
Rio de Plata	Argentina
Romana	Rome
Romaneie	Rumania
Sachsen	German state
Sard. Cyp.	Sardinia and Cyprus
Sax.	German state
Sede Vacante	Papal (Vatican)
Shqiperia*	Albania
Sic et Hier	Sicily
Sicil	Sicily
S. Marino	San Marino
Soloth	Swiss canton
Sonora	Mexico
Sud	Mexico
Sver	Sweden
Sveriges	Sweden
Thurgen	Swiss canton
Tigino	Swiss canton
Toscana	Italy
Tunisia	Tunis
Vargas	Mexico
Vaticano	Vatican City
Vaud	Swiss canton
Veneta	Italy
Westphalen	Germany
Wuertemberg	German state
Zamoscia	Poland
Zloti	Poland
Zuid-Afrikanische	South African Republic
Zurich	Swiss canton

TABLE B

Monetary Units and Countries Using Them

Monetary Unit	Nation of Issue
Anna	India
Balboa	Panama
Banu	Rumania
Belion	Morocco
Besa	Abyssinia or Eritrea
Bit	Virgin Islands
Bolivar	Venezuela
Boliviano	Bolivia
Cent	Newfoundland
	United States
	Canada
	Cuba
	Hawaii
	Puerto Rico
	British West Indies
	British Guiana
	British Honduras
	Dominican Republic
	Liberia
	Hong Kong
	China (Fen)
	Straits Settlements
	Federated Malay States
	Netherlands
	Ceylon
	British East Africa
	Zanzibar
	Somaliland (Italian)
Centavo	Portugal

Monetary Unit	Nation of Issue
Centavo (*cont.*)	
	Nicaragua
	Cuba
	Philippine Islands
	Salvador
	Mexico
	Peru
	Ecuador
	Argentina
	Honduras
	Bolivia
	Chile
	Guatemala
	Colombia
	Paraguay
Centesimo	Chile
	Uruguay
	Panama
	Italy
Centimo	Costa Rica
	Spain
	Venezuela
Centime	France
	Belgium
	Monaco
	Switzerland
	Haiti
	Indo-China
Colon	Salvador
	Costa Rica
Cordoba	Nicaragua
Dinar	Serbia or Persia
Dollar	Newfoundland
	United States

Monetary Unit	Nation of Issue
Dollar (cont.)	Hawaii
	Puerto Rico
	Canada
	British West Indies
	British Guiana
	British Honduras
	Dominican Republic
	Liberia
	Straits Settlements
	Federated Malay States
	Hong Kong
Drachma	Greece
Escudo	Portugal
Fen	China
Filler	Hungary
Florin	Netherlands
Franc	France
	Belgium
	Monaco
	Switzerland
Gourde	Haiti
Guilder	Netherlands
Heller	Austria
	German East Africa
Kopeck	Russia
Korona	Hungary
Kran	Persia
Krona	Sweden
	Iceland
Krone	Denmark
	Norway
	Austria
Lepton	Greece

Monetary Unit	Nation of Issue
Leu	Rumania
Lev	Bulgaria
Libra	Peru
Lira	Egypt
	Italy
	Turkey
Maria Theresa Thaler	Northeast Coast of Africa
Mark	Germany
Markka	Finland
Millieme	Egypt
Milreis	Brazil
	(old) Portugal
Ore	Denmark
	Sweden
	Norway
Para	Serbia
	Montenegro
	Egypt
	Turkey
Penni	Finland
Penny	United Kingdom
	Australia
	New Zealand
	British colonies
	United States
Perpera	Montenegro
Peseta	Spain
Peso	Argentina (gold and paper)
	Uruguay
	Chile
	Colombia
	Guatemala
	Paraguay

Monetary Unit	Nation of Issue
Peso (*cont.*)	
	Honduras
	Mexico
	Philippine Islands
	Panama (old half-Balboa)
	Cuba
Pfennig	Germany
Piastre	Egypt
	Turkey
	Indo-China
Pice	India
Pie	India
Pound (Sterling)	United Kingdom
	Australia
	New Zealand
	British colonies
Pound (Egyptian)	Egypt
Pound (Turkish)	Turkey
Reis (Real)	Brazil
	Portugal
Rial	Morocco
Rin	Japan
Rouble	Russia
Rupee	Ceylon
	British East Africa
	Zanzibar
	Italian Somaliland
	India
	German East Africa
Satang	Siam
Sen	Japan
Shahi	Persia
Shilling	United Kingdom
Sol	Peru

Monetary Unit	Nation of Issue
Stiver	Netherlands
Stotinka	Bulgaria
Sucre	Ecuador
Talari	Abyssinia
Tallero	Eritrea
Thaler (Maria Theresa)	Northeast Coast of Africa
Tical	Siam
Yen	Japan
Yuan	China

TABLE C

Countries and Monetary Units They Use

Issued by:	Monetary Unit
Abyssinia	Maria Theresa Dollar, Talan
Afghanistan	Rupee
Argentina	Peso
Austria	Krone
Belgium	Franc
Bolivia	Boliviano
Brazil	Milreis
British colonies	Pound
British East Africa	Rupee
British Honduras	Dollar
British West Indies	Dollar
Bulgaria	Lev
Canada	Dollar
Ceylon	Rupee
Chile	Peso
China	Yuan

Issued by:	Monetary Unit
Colombia	Peso
Costa Rica	Colon
Cuba	Peso
Denmark	Krone
Dominican Republic	United States Dollar
East Africa (ex-German)	Rupee
Ecuador	Sucre
Egypt	Egyptian Pound
Eritrea	Tallero
Finland	Markka
French Indo-China	Piastre
Germany	Mark
Great Britain	Pound Sterling
Greece	Drachma
Guatemala	Peso
Haiti	Gourde
Hawaii	United States Dollar
Honduras	Peso
Hong Kong	Dollar
Hungary	Korona
India	Rupee
Israel	Israel Pound
Italian Somaliland	Rupee
Italy	Lira
Japan	Yen
Java	Guilder
Korea	Yen
Liberia	United States Dollar
Malaya	Dollar
Mexico	Peso
Montenegro	Perpera
Monaco	Rial
Netherlands	Guilden
New Brunswick	Dollar

Issued by:	Monetary Unit
Newfoundland	Dollar
Nicaragua	Cordoba
Norway	Krone
Nova Scotia	Dollar
Panama	Balboa, Peso
Paraguay	Peso
Persia	Kran
Peru	Peruvian Pound
Philippine Islands	Peso
Puerto Rico	American Dollar
Portugal	Escudo
Rumania	Lev
Russia	Rouble
Salvador	Colon
Serbia	Dinar
Siam	Tical
Somaliland	Rupee
Spain	Peseta
Straits Settlements	Dollar
Sweden	Krona
Switzerland	Franc
Turkey	Piastre
Uruguay	Peso
Venezuela	Bolivar
Zanzibar	Rupee

TABLE D

Additional Place Names

Place Name	Location	Currency Used
Aden	Arabia	British
Algeria	Africa	French
Andorra	Europe	Spanish and French
Angola	Africa	Portuguese
Anguilla	West Indies	British
Antigua	West Indies	British
Arabia	Asia Minor	Turkish
Asuncion Island	Africa	British
Australia	Oceania	British
Azores	Atlantic Ocean	Portuguese
Bahamas	West Indies	British and United States
Barbados	West Indies	British and United States
Barbuda	West Indies	British
Basutoland	Africa	British
Bechuanaland	Africa	British
Bermuda	Atlantic Ocean	British and United States
Borneo (North)	Malaya	Straits Settlements
Borneo	Malaya	Dutch

Brunei	Malaya	Straits Settlements
Burma	India	Republic of Burma
Canal Zone	Central America	United States
Canary Islands	Africa	Spanish
Cape of Good Hope	Africa	British
Cape Verde Islands	Africa	Portuguese
Comoro Islands	Africa	French
Congo, Belgian	Africa	Belgian
Congo (French)	Africa	French
Congo (Portuguese)	Africa	Portuguese
Crete	Europe	Greek
Curacao	South America	Dutch
Cyprus	Asia Minor	British
Dahomey	Africa	French
Dominica	West Indies	British
Dominican Republic	West Indies	Dominican
East Africa (British)	Africa	British
East Africa (Portuguese)	Africa	Portuguese and British
Falkland Islands	South America	British
Fernando Po	Africa	Spanish
Formosa	China	Japanese
Gambia	Africa	British
Gibraltar	Europe	British and Spanish
Goa	India	Portuguese

55

TABLE D (*cont.*)

Place Name	Location	Currency Used
Gold Coast	Africa	British
Grenada	West Indies	British and United States
Guadeloupe	West Indies	French
Guam	Oceania	United States
Guiana (British)	South America	United States
Guiana (Dutch)	South America	Dutch
Guiana (French)	South America	French
Guinea (French)	Africa	French
Guinea (Portuguese)	Africa	Portuguese
Ivory Coast	Africa	French
Jamaica	West Indies	British
Kamerun	Africa	British
Labuan	Malaya	Straits Settlements
Liechtenstein	Europe	Austrian
Lourenco Marques	Africa	Portuguese and British
Luxemburg	Europe	French and German
Madagascar	Africa	French
Madeira	Africa	Portuguese
Macao	China	Portuguese
Malta	Europe	British
Marianne Islands	Oceania	British
Marshall Islands	Oceania	British
Martinique	West Indies	French

Mauritius	Indian Ocean	British
Mayotte	Africa	French
Monaco	Europe	French
Natal	Africa	British
Nevis	West Indies	British
New Caledonia	Oceania	French
New Guinea	Oceania	British
New Hebrides	Oceania	French
New Zealand	South Pacific Ocean	British
Niger	Africa	French
Nigeria	Africa	British
Nyasaland	Africa	British and Turkish
Orange River	Africa	British
Principe	Africa	Portuguese
Reunion	Africa	French
Rhodesia	Africa	British
Rio de Oro	Africa	Spanish
Rio Muni	Africa	Spanish
St. Christopher (St. Kitts)	West Indies	British
St. Helena	Africa	British
St. Lucia	West Indies	British
St. Thomas	West Indies	United States
St. Vincent	West Indies	British
Samoa (Tutuila)	Oceania	United States
Somoa (Sayai & Upolu)	Oceania	United States

TABLE D (*cont.*)

Place Name	Location	Currency Used
San Marino	Europe	Italian
Sarawak	East Indies	Straits Settlements
Senegal	Africa	French
Seychelles	Africa	British
Sierre Leone	Africa	British
Socotra	East Indies	British
Somali (Italian)	Africa	Italian
Somali (Coast)	Africa	French
Somali (British)	Africa	British
Sumatra	East Indies	Dutch
Surinam	South America	Dutch
Swaziland	Africa	British
Timor	Malaya	Portuguese
Togo (British)	Africa	British
Togo (French)	Africa	French
Tonga	Oceania	British
Transvaal	Africa	British
Trinidad	West Indies	British and United States
Upper Senegal	Africa	French
Tunisia	Africa	French
Turkestan	Asia	Turkish
Uganda	Africa	British
Virgin Islands	West Indies	British and United States
Zanzibar	Africa	British

TABLE E

Countries with Strange Languages

Abyssinia (see Ethiopia)
Afghanistan
Baroda
Bengal
Bombay
Burma
Celebes Island
China
Chinese Soviet
Chinese Turkestan
Comoro Islands
Egypt
Ethiopia
Georgia (in Russia)
Indian states
Iran
Israel
Japan
Korea
Madras

Manchukuo
Mongolia
Morocco
Nepal
Persia (see Iran)
Prince of Wales Island
Saudi Arabia
Siam (see Thailand)
Sudan
Sumatra
Syria
Thailand
Tibet
Tunisia
Turkey
Yemen
Zanzibar

CHAPTER 7

How to Collect Foreign Coins

If you want to collect foreign coins you can obtain names of dealers from the coin section of your local newspaper or hobby magazine, or from the telephone company's Classified Directory, or you can subscribe to coin magazines such as:

*World Coin News
Iola, Wisconsin 54945

The Numismatist
P.O. Box 2366
Colorado Springs, Colorado 80901

*Numismatic News
Iola, Wisconsin 54945

Coinage
17337 Ventura Blvd.
Encina, California 91316

*Coins Magazine
Iola, Wisconsin 54945

*Coin World
Sidney News Bldg.
Sidney, Ohio 45365

*Published weekly. Others are published monthly.

Be alert to collect specimens in the best possible condition, keeping in mind that the fun in this hobby consists of hunting for the coin you want.

As your collection becomes more valuable you should consult an insurance broker about buying protection against loss from fire and theft.

The question of cleaning your coins may come to mind. Do not try to clean a proof (a special coin issued for collectors) or an uncirculated coin, for you will only damage it. If, however, you wish to clean fine coins or coins in good condition, you may safely do so as follows:

Silver coins: Clean with bicarbonate of soda paste by rubbing gently and then washing off. You can also immerse silver coins in household ammonia and dry them gently.

Copper coins: Rub gently with a little oil in a chamois cloth. Never scrub them down to the raw copper. The oil and rubbing will take off the surface dirt.

For storing and exhibiting your collection, build your own cabinet and place the coins flat in the trays. Or keep them in the standard coin envelopes purchased from a dealer, filing them vertically in coin boxes (metal or cardboard) with all information written on the outside of the envelopes. Of course, you can also keep the collection in coin boards or in boards with cellulose acetate slides through which your coins will be visible from both sides. Some collectors use plastic holders in standard sizes or special ones made to order.

Keep in mind that the age of the coin does not make it valuable. The only factors that make a coin valuable are scarcity, state of preservation, and demand.

To profit from investment in foreign coins you need discrimination in making the original purchases. In general, foreign coins of silver-dollar size, if perfect in condition, steadily increase in value. Those of small countries with a limited issue of coins make the most substantial advances in value.

Foreign gold coins fluctuate in value more than silver coins do, according to popularity and demand. While there are times when foreign gold coins have increased in value, there have also been periods when their resale value has decreased to a point approaching the bullion value.

Important Note

The alphabetical listings in the following chapter cover foreign countries and their coinage up to 1980. By then, changes in valuations, types of metals used, and even the names of countries themselves, were occurring with increasing frequency. Such changes have been included, along with listings of new countries, thus enabling the collector to check the old against the new, as they stood at that time.

In the last decade, changes have become more far-reaching than ever. Along with new values and new metals, new nations have appeared with great rapidity; while even the most staid governments have abandoned tradition and switched their coinage to the decimal system, making it a whole new game from the collector's standpoint.

The collector should not expect the older coins to show a marked advance in "current worth." Those figures have been based on prices quoted by dealers whose supplies have in most instances been increased in anticipation of a future shortage of such items. But coin collecting, too, is expanding, which in itself can cause a scarcity of wanted items, for which the serious collector should be prepared.

CHAPTER 8

Foreign Coins by Countries

In the following pages the typical denominations of coins for each of many countries are shown. There are of course additional coins of different denominations and coins made of different metal. No claim to thorough coverage is made in a book of this size; merely, a broad outline is given on the subject in order to whet the reader's appetite for collecting.

Important Facts Regarding Modern Coins

The values stated are for typical coins, not for rarities. The designation crown means the size of the United States silver dollar.

The illustrations include coins of ancient origin or historical significance, because these are of special interest to collectors. The same applies to the early mintages of certain countries, which are also depicted. More modern coins are included, because they represent the types that new collectors are most likely to come across. These serve as a guide to other coins that are simply listed, as it is often quite easy to identify a coin by its similarity to a somewhat standard pattern.

In certain countries, the principal changes are in the heads of ruling monarchs. This is especially true in many British colonies. These changes naturally cause a variation in value to collectors, the coins of older mintage ordinarily commanding higher prices than the newer, except when other factors enter to cause a scarcity.

Inasmuch as the average collector is likely to acquire the newer or commoner types, the current prices quoted are for such coins. Any bearing dates in the 1800s or early 1900s should be checked more carefully on the chance that they are worth more than average quotations even if they do not rate as actual rarities.

Prior to World War I and the years immediately following, many countries minted gold coins, while others were on the silver standard. Much of their coinage was in silver, sometimes down to surprisingly low values. But as they went off these standards or relaxed their requirements, token currencies were introduced. Because of their rarity, coins of nickel, brass, aluminum and various alloys may command high figures among collectors. But often, the new coinage was the result of an inflationary trend, giving it less worth.

In some of the following listings, values are given in descending order, with mention of different metals and alloys as they occur. These are generally of widely separated dates, so the reader should bear that point in mind, recognizing that the "cheaper" coins are usually the newer. In some instances, the variance is so marked—due to the drop in value of the monetary unit involved—that two sets of listings have been given, the first representing the original currency, the next its later and much depleted value.

In many cases, there has been a change in name of monetary units. Here, again, the original is given first, while the newer values follow. This is not always a sign of inflation; there are instances where the currency has been stabilized or a new form established. The current worth of such coins is often an index to that factor.

Changes of government also produce changes in currency as well as the appearance of the coins themselves. Colonies become independent and new nations have been formed in increasing numbers during recent years. Effort has been made to include all these in the alphabetical listing, with reference to their former status.

Quotations of current worth are merely approximate and refer to coins that are in very good to very fine condition. With older coins, those of good condition may be hard enough to find, but more recent coins should be of fine condition to rate as collector's items. Odd dates, slight variations and many other factors may increase the value of a seemingly common coin, so that, too, is something not to be overlooked.

ABYSSINIA
(See Ethiopia)

AFGHANISTAN

Coins		Current Worth
5 Afghani	Aluminum	$ 5
5 Afghani	Nickel-clad	$ 3
2 Afghani	Aluminum	$ 2.50
2 Afghani	Nickel-clad	$ 1.50
1 Afghani	Nickel-clad	$ 1
50 Puli	Nickel-clad	50¢
50 Puli	Bronze	75¢
25 Puli	Nickel-clad	75¢
25 Puli	Copper-nickel	75¢
25 Puli	Bronze	60¢
10 Puli	Copper-nickel	60¢
10 Puli	Bronze	50¢
5 Puli	Bronze	35¢
3 Puli	Bronze	60¢
2 Puli	Bronze	35¢
1 Puli	Bronze	85¢

The rugged, mountainous monarchy of Afghanistan is situated in southwest Asia, where it is almost completely hemmed in by Iran, the U.S.S.R. and Pakistan, except for a narrow corridor between the last two, stretching to the western boundary of China.

ALBANIA

Coins		Current Worth
100 Franka Ari	Gold	$700
50 Franka Ari	Gold	$350
20 Franka Ari	Gold	$160
10 Franka Ari	Gold	$ 80
2 Franka Ari	Silver	$ 25
1 Franka Ari	Silver	$ 10

Coinage of Republic

10 Lek (2 Franka Ari)	Silver	$ 65
5 Lek (1 Franka Ari)	Silver	$ 35
5 Lek	Zinc	$ 2
2 Lek	Zinc	85¢
1 Lek	Zinc	75¢
Half Lek	Zinc	60¢
1 Lek	Aluminum	$ 1.75
50 Quindarka	Aluminum	$ 1.50
20 Quindarka	Aluminum	$ 1
10 Quindarka	Aluminum	60¢
5 Quindarka	Aluminum	50¢

Albania is a Balkan Communist republic that runs for 225 miles along the east coast of the Adriatic Sea. It is bounded on the north and east by Yugoslavia and on the south by Greece. Albania, which is narrow and mountainous, is a little larger than the state of Vermont.

ALGERIA

Coins		Current Worth
100 Francs	Nickel	$ 1.50
50 Francs	Nickel	75¢
10 Francs	Nickel	40¢

Coinage Minted by the Algerian Republic:

10 Dinars	Bronze	$ 4
5 Dinars	Bronze	$ 2
5 Dinars	Silver	$ 15
1 Dinar	Copper-Nickel	85¢
50 Centimes	Aluminum-Bronze	50¢
20 Centimes	Aluminum-Bronze	35¢
10 Centimes	Aluminum-Bronze	25¢
5 Centimes	Aluminum	20¢
2 Centimes	Aluminum	15¢
1 Centime	Aluminum	10¢

The new Republic of Algeria, formerly an integral part of France, became independent in 1962, but already had its own limited coinage. Located in North Africa, Algeria extends 640 miles along the Mediterranean Sea. It is bounded by Morocco on the west and Tunisia on the east. Algeria extends 350 miles southward into the Sahara Desert.

ANGOLA

Coins		Current Worth
20 Escudos	Silver	$ 7.50
20 Escudos	Copper-Nickel	$ 4.50
10 Escudos	Silver	$ 4
10 Escudos	Copper-Nickel	$ 2
2 1/2 Escudos	Copper-Nickel	$ 1
1 Escudo	Bronze	50¢
50 Centavos	Nickel	50¢
50 Centavos	Bronze	25¢
20 Centavos	Bronze	25¢
10 Centavos	Bronze	15¢

Known also as Portuguese West Africa, Angola is a Portuguese overseas province that runs 1000 miles south from the Congo river, along the west coast of Africa. It became the People's Republic of Angola after independence was declared in 1975.

ANGUILLA

Coins		Current Worth
20 Dollars	Gold	$250
10 Dollars	Gold	$135
5 Dollars	Gold	$ 50
4 Dollars	Silver	$ 35
2 Dollars	Silver	$ 25
1 Dollar	Silver	$ 15
Half Dollar	Silver	$ 10

Liberty dollars stamped with date range from $35 to $750 according to rarity.

ARGENTINA

Coins		Current Worth
1 Peso	Silver	$ 50
50 Centavos	Silver	$ 12
20 Centavos	Silver	$ 5
10 Centavos	Silver	$ 2.50
10 Pesos	Nickel-clad	75¢
5 Pesos	Nickel-clad	60¢
1 Peso	Nickel-clad	50¢
50 Centavos	Nickel-clad	50¢
20 Centavos	Copper-Nickel	30¢
10 Centavos	Copper-Nickel	20¢
5 Centavos	Copper-Nickel	15¢

Peso, or 8 Reales (Silver), 1813, worth $100

Decimo of Buenos Ayres (Copper), 1822, worth $3

5/10 Decimo of Buenos Ayres, 1827, worth $5

2 Centavos (Copper), 1890, worth $350

The Argentine Republic extends from Bolivia 2,300 miles to
Cape Horn and from the ridge of the Andes to the South Atlantic,
occupying the greater part of southern South America. It is
bounded by Bolivia on the north, by Paraguay on the northeast,
by Brazil, Uruguay and the Atlantic Ocean on the east, and by
Chile on the west.

ARGENTINA

Coins		Current Worth

Later Currency (1960 on), with 12-sided coins:

25 Pesos		
(Commemorative)	Steel	$ 1
25 Pesos	Steel	75¢

ARGENTINA (*cont.*)

Coins		Current Worth
10 Pesos		
(Commemorative)	Steel	75¢
10 Pesos	Steel	60¢
5 Pesos	Steel	50¢

Circular Coinage (1957 and later)

1 Peso		
(Commemorative)	Steel	75¢
1 Peso	Aluminum-Brass	50¢

Regular Coinage

Coins		Current Worth
1 Peso	Steel	50¢
50 Centavos	Steel	35¢
20 Centavos	Steel	25¢
10 Centavos	Steel	20¢
5 Centavos	Steel	15¢

World Soccer Coinage (1977)

Coins		Current Worth
3000 Pesos	Silver	$ 25
2000 Pesos	Silver	$ 17.50
1000 Pesos	Silver	$ 9
100 Pesos	Aluminum-Bronze	$ 1.50
50 Pesos	Mixed Metals	$ 1.50
20 Pesos	Mixed Metals	75¢

AUSTRALIA

Coins		Current Worth
Sovereign	Gold	$250
Half Sovereign	Gold	$150
Crown (5 shillings)	Silver	$ 30
Florin (2 shillings)	Silver	$ 12.50
Shilling	Silver	$ 6.00
6 pence	Silver	$ 3
3 pence	Silver	$ 1.50
Penny	Bronze	25¢
Halfpenny	Bronze	15¢

Decimal system (1966 and later)

Coins		Current Worth
200 Dollars	Gold	$300
50 Cents	Silver	$ 12.50
50 Cents	Copper-Nickel (12-sided)	$ 1.25
20 Cents	Copper-Nickel	60¢
10 Cents	Copper-Nickel	30¢
5 Cents	Copper-Nickel	20¢
2 Cents	Bronze	15¢
1 Cent	Bronze	10¢

The continent of Australia is situated between 10° 41' (or, if you include Tasmania, 43° 39') south latitude, and 113° 9' to 153° 39' east longitude in the Pacific Ocean on the east and south.

AUSTRIA

Coins		Current Worth
100 Kronen	Gold	$700
20 Kronen	Gold	$135
10 Kronen	Gold	$ 67.50

AUSTRIA (*cont.*) Coins		Current Worth
5 Kronen	Silver	$ 22.50
2 Kronen	Silver	$ 2.50
1 Krona	Silver	$ 4.50
20 Heller	Nickel	60¢
10 Heller	Nickel	30¢
2 Heller	Copper	20¢
1 Heller	Copper	20¢
Coinage After World War I		
25 Schilling	Gold	$135
1 Schilling	Silver	$ 6
Half Schilling	Silver	$ 3
50 Groschen	Copper-Nickel	$ 1
10 Groschen	Copper-Nickel	25¢
5 Groschen	Copper-Nickel	20¢
2 Groschen	Bronze	10¢
1 Groschen	Bronze	10¢
Coinage After World War II		
10 Schilling	Silver	$ 6.50
10 Schilling	Copper-Nickel	$ 1.50
5 Schilling	Silver	$ 3.25
5 Schilling	Aluminum	$ 2.50
5 Schilling	Copper-Nickel	$ 1
2 Schilling	Aluminum	$ 1.50
1 Schilling	Aluminum	50¢
1 Schilling	Aluminum-Bronze	50¢
50 Groschen	Aluminum	25¢
50 Groschen	Aluminum-Bronze	25¢
20 Groschen	Aluminum-Bronze	25¢
10 Groschen	Aluminum	20¢
10 Groschen	Zinc	20¢
5 Groschen	Zinc	20¢
2 Groschen	Aluminum	20¢
1 Groschen	Zinc	15¢

Austria in Central Europe is bounded on the north by
Czechoslovakia, on the east by Hungary, on the south by Italy and
Yugoslavia, and on the west by Germany, Switzerland and Liech-
tenstein.

4 Ducats (Gold), about 1900, worth $500

1 Kreuzer (Copper), 1816, worth $4.50

Modern Commemorative Coinage:

Over a period of 10 years beginning with 1928, silver commemorative coins were struck, honoring famous Austrians. These
were of 2 schillings in value and today are worth up to $50 each in
uncirculated condition.

A later and more numerous series of commemorative coins
was instituted in 1955 and is still in progress. These coins relate

more to historic events than to personalities, though the latter are included. All to date are struck in silver, the earliest being of 25 schillings in value, worth from $12.50 to $25 in uncirculated condition; the rest are 50 schillings in value, worth from $15 to $30.

BAHAMA ISLANDS

Coins		Current Worth
250 Dollars	Gold	$400
200 Dollars	Gold	$250
150 Dollars	Gold	$175
100 Dollars	Gold	$200
50 Dollars	Gold	$135
25 Dollars	Gold	$ 60
10 Dollars	Gold	$ 45
10 Dollars	Silver	$ 45
5 Dollars	Silver	$ 40
2 Dollars	Silver	$ 30
1 Dollar	Silver	$ 15
50 Cents	Silver	$ 7.50
25 Cents	Nickel	75¢
15 Cents (Square)	Copper-Nickel	50¢
10 Cents (Scalloped)	Copper-Nickel	35¢
5 Cents	Copper-Nickel	20¢
1 Cent	Brass	10¢

The Bahamas comprise almost 700 islands off the coast of the United States in the Atlantic ocean near Florida.

BAHRAIN

Coins		Current Worth
100 Dinars	Gold	$550
10 Dinars	Gold	$350
250 Fils	Copper-Nickel	$ 3
500 Fils (5 Dinars)	Silver	$ 5
100 Fils (1 Dinar)	Copper-Nickel	$ 2
50 Fils	Copper-Nickel	$ 1
25 Fils	Copper-Nickel	50¢
10 Fils	Bronze	35¢
5 Fils	Bronze	25¢
1 Fil	Bronze	15¢

The tiny achipelago of Bahrain is situated in the Persian Gulf, just off the coast of Saudi Arabia. A British protectorate since 1820, Bahrain was nominally under the rule of a series of sheiks. The country introduced its own currency in 1965 and announced its independence in 1971.

BANGLADESH

Coins		Current Worth
1 Taka	Copper-Nickel	50¢
50 Poisha	Steel	30¢
50 Poisha	Copper-Nickel	65¢
25 Poisha	Steel	45¢
25 Poisha	Copper-Nickel	20¢
10 Poisha	Aluminum	35¢
5 Poisha	Aluminum	25¢
1 Poisha	Aluminum	15¢

Bangladesh was formerly the eastern zone of Pakistan, but became an independent nation in 1971 and adopted its new coinage (100 Poisha = 1 Taka) in 1973.

Bangladesch

BARBADOS

(See British Caribbean Territories)

Coins		Current Worth
Penny	Copper	$ 12.50
Halfpenny	Copper	$ 12.50

Barbados is the most eastern of the West Indies, lying out in the Atlantic at 13° north latitude.

Penny (Copper), 1788, worth $12.50

Halfpenny (Copper), 1792, worth $12.50

BARBADOS

Decimal Values

Coins		Current Worth
10 Dollars	Silver	$ 35
10 Dollars	Copper-Nickel	$ 15
5 Dollars	Silver	$ 17.50
5 Dollars	Copper-Nickel	$ 12.50
2 Dollars	Copper-Nickel	$ 3.50
1 Dollar	Copper-Nickel	$ 2
25 Cents	Copper-Nickel	75¢
10 Cents	Copper-Nickel	35¢
5 Cents	Brass	20¢
1 Cent	Bronze	10¢

BELGIAN CONGO

Coins		Current Worth
50 Francs	Silver	$ 65
5 Francs	Nickel	$ 2.50
1 Franc	Nickel	$ 1.50
50 Centimes	Nickel	$ 1.25

BELGIAN CONGO (*cont.*)

Coins		Current Worth
20 Centimes	Nickel	50¢
10 Centimes	Nickel	$ 1
5 Centimes	Nickel	$ 1
2 Centimes	Copper	$ 2.50
1 Centime	Bronze	$ 1

The Belgian Congo had a short coast line on the south Atlantic Ocean at the mouth of the Congo, where the Port of Banana is situated in a fine natural harbor. French Equatorial Africa lies to the north and west, Angola to the south, Tanganyika and Uganda to the east, and the Sudan to the north. In 1960, this former Belgian colony became the new Republic of Congo.

2 Centimes (Copper), 1888, worth $2.50

BELGIUM

Coins		Current Worth
20 Francs	Gold	$135
5 Francs	Silver	$ 22.50
2 Francs	Silver	$ 8.50
1 Franc	Silver	$ 4.75
50 Centimes	Silver	$ 2.50
25 Centimes	Nickel	25¢

BELGIUM (*cont.*)

Coins		Current Worth
10 Centimes	Nickel	15¢
5 Centimes	Nickel	15¢
2 Centimes	Copper	15¢
1 Centime	Copper	15¢
4 Belgas (20 Francs)	Nickel	$ 25
2 Belgas	Nickel	$ 22.50
1 Belga	Nickel	$ 2.50
2 Francs	Nickel	50¢
1 Franc	Nickel	25¢
250 Francs	Silver	$250
100 Francs	Silver	$ 15
50 Francs	Silver	$ 10
20 Francs	Silver	$ 6
5 Francs	Copper-Nickel	50¢
1 Franc	Copper-Nickel	20¢
50 Centimes	Copper	10¢
20 Centimes	Copper	10¢

Belgium is bounded on the north by the Netherlands and the North Sea, on the east by Germany and Luxemburg, on the south by France, and on the west by France and the North Sea.

5 Centimes (Copper), 1857, worth $2.50

10 Centimes (Nickel), 1902, worth 30¢

50 Francs (Silver), 1939, worth $12

BELIZE

(Formerly British Honduras)

Coins		Current Worth
10 Dollars	Silver	$ 35
10 Dollars	Copper-Nickel	$ 25
5 Dollars	Copper-Nickel	$ 15
1 Dollar	Copper-Nickel	$ 7.50
50 Cents	Copper-Nickel	$ 1
25 Cents	Copper-Nickel	50¢
10 Cents	Copper-Nickel	35¢
5 Cents	Copper-Nickel	25¢
1 Cent	Bronze	15¢

BERMUDA

Decimal Values

Coins		Current Worth
1 Crown (Commemorative)	Silver	$ 15
1 Penny (Dated 1793)	Copper	$ 30
250 Dollars	Gold	$450
100 Dollars	Gold	$150
50 Dollars	Gold	$ 80
25 Dollars	Silver	$ 45
25 Dollars	Copper-Nickel	$ 35
20 Dollars	Gold	$800
1 Dollar	Silver	$ 35
50 Cents	Copper-Nickel	$ 1
25 Cents	Copper-Nickel	50¢
10 Cents	Copper-Nickel	25¢
5 Cents	Copper-Nickel	15¢
1 Cent	Bronze	10¢

BHUTAN

Coins		Current Worth
5 Sertum	Gold	$1000
2 Sertum	Gold	$ 500
1 Sertum	Gold	$ 200
3 Rupees	Copper-Nickel	$ 4
1 Rupee	Copper-Nickel	$ 1.50
Half Rupee	Silver	$ 15
Half Rupee	Nickel	$ 3.50
50 Naiya Paisa	Copper-Nickel	$ 1
25 Naiya Paisa	Copper-Nickel	50¢
1 Pice	Bronze	$ 1.50

BHUTAN (*cont.*)

Coins		Current Worth
New Coinage (1974)		
30 Ngultrums	Silver	$ 15
15 Ngultrums	Silver	$ 12
3 Ngultrums	Copper-Nickel	$ 5
1 Ngultrum	Copper-Nickel	75¢
50 Chetrums	Copper-Nickel	$ 3
25 Chetrums	Copper-Nickel	35¢
20 Chetrums	Copper-Nickel	25¢
10 Chetrums	Aluminum	25¢
5 Chetrums	Aluminum	15¢

Bhutan is an Asiatic kingdom situated high in the Himalaya Mountains, bounded by Sikkim on the west, Tibet (China) on the north, with India on the south and east. It is also called Druk-Yul.

BIAFRA

Coins		Current Worth
25 Pounds	Gold	$1600
10 Pounds	Gold	$ 800
5 Pounds	Gold	$ 350
2 Pounds	Gold	$ 180
1 Pound	Gold	$ 100
1 Pound	Silver	$ 20
2 1/2 Shillings	Aluminum	$ 2
1 Shilling	Aluminum	$ 1.50
3 Pence	Bronze	$ 5

Biafra was the name given to the eastern portion of the Republic of Nigeria, during a brief period of independence between the years 1967–70.

BOLIVIA

Coins		Current Worth
10 Bolivianos	Bronze	$ 1.25
5 Bolivianos	Bronze	$ 1
1 Boliviano	Bronze	75¢
1 Boliviano	Silver	$ 22.50
50 Centavos	Silver	$ 10
20 Centavos	Silver	$ 5
10 Centavos	Copper-Nickel	50¢
5 Centavos	Copper-Nickel	35¢

Bolivia is bounded by Peru and Chile on the west, Brazil on the north and east, Paraguay on the east, and Argentina on the south. It lies across the Andes.

8 Sueldos (Silver), 1845, worth $50

1 Boliviano (Silver), worth $30

10 Centavos (Nickel), 1907, worth $1.25

BOLIVIA
Reformed Currency (1965)

Coins		Current Worth
500 Pesos Bolivianos	Silver	$ 35
250 Pesos	Silver	$ 17.50
100 Pesos	Silver	$ 10
5 Pesos	Nickel-clad Steel	$ 1.50
1 Peso	Nickel-clad Steel	$ 1
50 Centavos	Nickel-clad Steel	60¢
25 Centavos	Nickel-clad Steel	50¢
20 Centavos	Nickel-clad Steel	35¢
10 Centavos	Copper-clad Steel	20¢
5 Centavos	Copper-clad Steel	15¢

BOTSWANA

Coins		Current Worth
150 Pula	Gold	$350
10 Pula	Silver	$ 25
5 Pula	Silver	$ 15
1 Pula	Copper-Nickel	$ 2.50
50 Thebe	Copper-Nickel	$ 1.25
25 Thebe	Copper-Nickel	75¢
10 Thebe	Copper-Nickel	35¢
5 Thebe	Bronze	25¢
1 Thebe	Aluminum	15¢
50 Cents	Silver (Commemorative, 1966)	$ 10

Formerly the British Protectorate of Bechuanaland, the present Republic of Botswana is bounded by Rhodesia, South Africa and Southwest Africa. It also uses South African coins and currency.

50 Cents (Silver), 1966, worth $7.50

BRAZIL

Coins		Current Worth
20 Milreis	Gold	$550
10 Milreis	Gold	$400
2 Milreis	Silver	$ 20
1 Milreis (100 Reis)	Silver	$ 10
500 Reis	Silver	$ 6.50
400 Reis	Copper-Nickel	$ 1.50
300 Reis	Copper-Nickel	$ 1
200 Reis	Copper-Nickel	50¢
100 Reis	Copper-Nickel	30¢
50 Reis	Copper-Nickel	35¢
40 Reis	Bronze	50¢
20 Reis	Bronze	65¢
20 Reis	Copper-Nickel	35¢
5 Cruzeiros	Aluminum-Bronze	$ 1.50
2 Cruzeiros	Aluminum-Bronze	75¢
1 Cruzeiro	Aluminum-Bronze	50¢
50 Centavos	Aluminum	25¢
20 Centavos	Aluminum	20¢
10 Centavos	Aluminum	15¢

Brazil has a coast line on the Atlantic Ocean of 4889 miles and extends approximately 2676 miles from north to south and 2794 miles from east to west. It is bounded on the north by Venezuela and Dutch, British and French Guianas; on the east by the Atlantic Ocean; on the south by Uruguay, Argentine and Paraguay; on the west by Bolivia, Peru and Colombia. The northern part is the great heavily-wooded basin of the Amazon, which rises in the Peruvian Andes and empties into the Atlantic at the Equator.

Early Brazilian dollar-size pieces show at least part of a design from an earlier striking. The entire issue of 960 Reis pieces from 1810 to 1826 was struck over Spanish colonial coins.

BRAZIL

Coinage of 1965

Coins		Current Worth
50 Cruzeiros	Copper-Nickel	50¢
20 Cruzeiros	Aluminum	30¢
10 Cruzeiros	Aluminum	20¢

Reformed Currency (1967)

1 Cruzeiro	Nickel	$ 1.50
50 Centavos	Nickel	$ 1
20 Centavos	Copper-Nickel	35¢
10 Centavos	Copper-Nickel	25¢
5 Centavos	Stainless Steel	20¢
2 Centavos	Stainless Steel	10¢
1 Centavo	Stainless Steel	10¢

Commemorative Coinage (1970)

Coins		Current Worth
300 Cruzeiros	Gold	$300
20 Cruzeiros	Silver	$ 25
1 Cruzeiro	Nickel	$ 1.50

640 Reis (2/3 Dollar) (Silver), 1787, worth $25

2000 Reis (Silver), 1889, worth $32.50

500 Reis (Nickel), 1889, worth $10

BRITISH CARIBBEAN TERRITORIES

Includes Barbados, British Guiana, Leeward Islands, Trinidad, Tobago and Windward Islands.

Coins		Current Worth
50 Cents	Nickel	$ 1.75
25 Cents	Nickel	50¢
10 Cents	Nickel	40¢
5 Cents	Brass	30¢
2 Cents	Copper	20¢
1 Cent	Copper	15¢
Half Cent	Copper	$ 1

BRITISH EAST AFRICA,
EAST AFRICA, and UGANDA
Coins and Paper same as for Great Britain

Kenya Crown Colony and Protectorate extends from the Indian Ocean northeast to Somaliland, north to Ethiopia, west to Uganda, and south to Tanganyika.

The Uganda Protectorate lies to the west of Kenya with the Anglo-Egyptian Sudan on the north, Belgian Congo on the west, and Tanganyika on the south.

See Tanganyika Territory.

BRITISH GUIANA
(See British Caribbean Territories)

Coins— Same as for England, plus		Current Worth
1 Stiver	Copper	$ 5
Half Stiver	Copper	$ 3.50

British Guiana is on the north shore of South America.

Stiver (Copper), 1813, worth $5

BRITISH HONDURAS

Coins		Current Worth
50 Cents	Silver	$ 25
25 Cents	Silver	$ 12.50
10 Cents	Silver	$ 5
5 Cents	Copper-Nickel	$ 2
1 Cent	Bronze	50¢
50 Cents	Copper-Nickel	$ 1.50
25 Cents	Copper-Nickel	75¢
10 Cents	Copper-Nickel	50¢
5 Cents	Nickel-Brass	35¢
1 Cent	Bronze (scalloped edge)	20¢

British Honduras is in Central America on the Caribbean Sea, south of Yucatan.

50 Cents (Silver), 1911, worth $25

BRITISH NORTH BORNEO

Coins		Current Worth
25 Cents	Silver	$ 10
5 Cents	Nickel	$ 1
2 1/2 Cents	Nickel	$ 1
1 Cent	Nickel	50¢
1 Cent	Copper	50¢
Half Cent	Copper	$ 2

British North Borneo is a Crown Colony in the Malay Archipelago, formerly administered by a chartered company.

One Cent (Copper), 1882–1894, worth $2.50

BRITISH VIRGIN ISLANDS

Coins		Current Worth
100 Dollars	Gold	$160
25 Dollars	Gold	$ 50
25 Dollars	Silver	$ 50
5 Dollars	Silver	$ 50
5 Dollars	Copper-Nickel	$ 10
1 Dollar	Silver	$ 25
1 Dollar	Copper-Nickel	$ 7.50
50 Cents	Copper-Nickel	$ 2
25 Cents	Copper-Nickel	75¢

BRITISH VIRGIN ISLANDS (*cont.*)

Coins		Current Worth
10 Cents	Copper-Nickel	40¢
5 Cents	Copper-Nickel	25¢
1 Cent	Bronze	15¢

The British Virgin islands are a group consisting of three dozen islands in the West Indies, situated east of Puerto Rico.

BRITISH WEST AFRICA
Gambia, Gold Coast, Nigeria, Sierra Leone
(See also Ghana and Nigeria)

Coins		Current Worth
2 Shillings	Silver	$ 12.50
2 Shillings	Brass	$ 2
1 Shilling	Silver	$ 6
1 Shilling	Brass	$ 1.25
6 Pence	Silver	$ 3.50
6 Pence	Brass	$ 1
3 Pence	Silver	$ 2.50
3 Pence	Copper-Nickel	75¢
1 Penny	Copper-Nickel	60¢
1 Penny	Bronze	35¢
Half Penny	Copper-Nickel	50¢
Half Penny	Bronze	35¢
Tenth Penny	Copper-Nickel	50¢
Tenth Penny	Aluminum	75¢

This was a group of former British colonies supplied with a common currency that became obsolete after 1958.

BRUNEI

Coins		Current Worth
1000 Dollars	Gold	$1250
750 Dollars	Gold	$ 375
50 Dollars	Silver	$ 65
10 Dollars	Silver	$ 50
1 Dollar	Copper-Nickel	$ 15
50 Sen	Copper-Nickel	75¢
20 Sen	Copper-Nickel	50¢
10 Sen	Copper-Nickel	25¢
5 Sen	Copper-Nickel	15¢
1 Sen	Bronze	10¢

Brunei is a British protected Sultanate situated on the north-west coast of Borneo, fronting on the South China Sea.

BULGARIA

Coins		Current Worth
100 Leva	Gold	$750
20 Leva	Gold	$185
10 Leva	Gold	$135
5 Leva	Silver	$ 25
2 Leva	Silver	$ 15
1 Lev ·	Silver	$ 5
50 Stotinki	Silver	$ 2.50
20 Stotinki	Copper-Nickel	50¢
10 Stotinki	Copper-Nickel	35¢
5 Stotinki	Copper-Nickel	25¢
2 Stotinki	Bronze	$ 1.25
1 Stotinka	Bronze	$ 1.25

BULGARIA (*cont.*)

Coins		Current Worth
Revised Currency (1962)		
1 Lev	Nickel-Brass	$ 1.50
50 Stotinki	Nickel-Brass	$ 1
20 Stotinki	Nickel-Brass	60¢
10 Stotinki	Nickel-Brass	50¢
5 Stotinki	Brass	25¢
2 Stotinki	Brass	20¢
1 Stotinki	Brass	15¢

The Republic of Bulgaria is bounded on the north by Rumania, on the west by Yugoslavia, on the south by Greece, on the east by the Black Sea, and on the southeast by Turkey.

20 Stotinki (Nickel), 1888, worth $2.50

BURMA

Coins		Current Worth
8 Annas	Nickel	$ 5
4 Annas	Nickel	$ 3
2 Annas	Copper	$ 1.25
1 Anna	Copper	75¢
1/2 Anna	Copper	50¢

BURMA (*cont.*) Coins		Current Worth
	Decimal Coinage	
1 Kyat	Copper-Nickel	$ 1.50
50 Pyas	Copper-Nickel	75¢
25 Pyas	Copper-Nickel	40¢
10 Pyas	Copper-Nickel	25¢
5 Pyas	Copper-Nickel	15¢
1 Pya	Copper	10¢
	Later Coinage	
50 Pyas	Aluminum	$ 1
25 Pyas	Aluminum	50¢
10 Pyas	Aluminum	30¢
5 Pyas	Aluminum	20¢
1 Pya	Aluminum	15¢

The Union of Burma is a republic in the western part of the Indo-Chinese peninsula. It follows the Bay of Bengal and is bounded on the north and east by China, on the west by India and Pakistan, on the east by China, Laos and Thailand. Until 1937, Burma was administered by British India and it remained a part of the British Commonwealth until 1948.

In 1949 it issued its own currency based on the Anna system of India, but in 1952 it adopted the decimal system with 1 Kyat equalling 100 Pyas. All coins of less value than the Kyat were stamped from aluminum in 1966.

BURUNDI

Coins		Current Worth
500 Francs	Silver	$ 20
100 Francs	Gold	$650
50 Francs	Gold	$325

BURUNDI (*cont.*) Coins		Current Worth
25 Francs	Gold	$160
20 Francs	Gold	$150
10 Francs	Gold	$ 65
10 Francs	Copper-Nickel	$ 1.50
5 Francs	Aluminum	75¢
1 Franc	Aluminum	50¢
1 Franc	Brass	75¢

Burundi is an African Republic bounded by Rwanda, Tanzania and the Democratic Republic of Congo. It also has a shoreline along Lake Tanganyika. The country gained independence in 1962 and became a republic four years later.

CAMBODIA

Coins		Current Worth
50 Centimes	Aluminum	$ 3.50
20 Centimes	Aluminum	$ 2.50
10 Centimes	Aluminum	$ 1.25
50 Sen	Aluminum	$ 2
20 Sen	Aluminum	$ 1.50
10 Sen	Aluminum	$ 1

Cambodia was an Asiatic kingdom situated on the Gulf of Siam and bounded by Laos, Thailand and Vietnam. Formerly part of French Indo-China, it declared its independence in 1953.

CAMEROONS

Coins		Current Worth
100 Francs	Nickel	$ 3.50
50 Francs	Copper-Nickel	$ 2.50

For coinage less than 50 Francs see Equitorial African States.

The Federal Republic of Cameroons is on the West Coast of Africa, with Nigeria on the north, Central African Republic on the east and Congo on the south.

CANADA

Coins		Current Worth
10 Dollars	Gold	$375
5 Dollars	Gold	$200
1 Dollar	Silver	$ 25
50 Cents	Silver	$ 10
25 Cents	Silver	$ 5
20 Cents	Silver	$ 65
10 Cents	Silver	$ 2.50
5 Cents	Silver	$ 2.50
5 Cents	Nickel	25¢
1 Cent	Bronze	5¢ to 35¢
1 Cent (Large)	Bronze	75¢ to $2

New Coinage (1968 on)

Coins		Current Worth
100 Dollars	Gold	$250
50 Dollars	Gold	$250
20 Dollars	Gold	$250
10 Dollars	Silver	$ 15
5 Dollars	Silver	$ 7.50
1 Dollar	Nickel	$ 1.50
50 Cents	Nickel	75¢
25 Cents	Nickel	40¢
10 Cents	Nickel	15¢

The Dominion of Canada occupies the northern half of North America extending from the Atlantic to the Pacific Ocean.

Side View of One Penny Token (Copper), 1839, worth $200

One Cent (Copper), 1870–1901, worth $1.50

Front View of Half Penny Token (Copper), 1842, worth $2.50

CAPE VERDE

Coins		Current Worth
2,500 Escudos	Gold	$250
250 Escudos	Silver	$ 25
50 Escudos	Copper-Nickel	$ 5
20 Escudos	Copper-Nickel	$ 3
10 Escudos	Copper-Nickel	$ 2.50
10 Escudos	Silver	$ 8.50
5 Escudos	Nickel-Bronze	$ 1.75
2 1/2 Escudos	Nickel-Bronze	$ 1.75
1 Escudo	Nickel-Bronze	$ 1.50
50 Centavos	Nickel-Bronze	$ 1
20 Centavos	Bronze	$ 1
10 Centavos	Bronze	$ 1
5 Centavos	Bronze	$ 1

(Later Dates)

50 Centavos	Aluminum	75¢
20 Centavos	Aluminum	35¢

The Cape Verde Islands were a Portuguese overseas province about 500 miles off the coast of West Africa until they became independent in 1975.

CAYMAN ISLANDS

Coins		Current Worth
100 Dollars	Gold	$300
50 Dollars	Silver	$100
25 Dollars	Gold	$165
25 Dollars	Silver	$ 50
5 Dollars	Silver	$ 40
2 Dollars	Silver	$ 25
1 Dollar	Silver	$ 20
50 Cents	Silver	$ 12.50

CAYMAN ISLANDS (*cont.*)

Coins		Current Worth
25 Cents	Copper-Nickel	75¢
10 Cents	Copper-Nickel	30¢
5 Cents	Copper-Nickel	20¢
1 Cent	Bronze	10¢

The Cayman Islands are a group of the British West Indies, situated northwest of Jamaica.

CEYLON

Coins		Current Worth
5 Rupees	Silver	$ 27.50
1 Rupee	Copper-Nickel	$ 1.50
50 Cents	Silver	$ 6.50
25 Cents	Silver	$ 3.25
10 Cents	Silver	$ 2
5 Cents	Copper-Nickel	$ 1
1 Cent	Copper	$ 1.25
Half Cent	Copper	$ 1.25
Quarter Cent	Copper	$ 1.25

Later Issues

2 Rupees	Copper-Nickel	$ 2
50 Cents	Copper-Nickel	50¢
25 Cents	Copper-Nickel	30¢
10 Cents	Nickel-Brass	25¢
5 Cents	Nickel-Brass	15¢
2 Cents	Aluminum	15¢
1 Cent	Aluminum	15¢

(Some varieties of these values are square instead of round, while others have wavy edges.)

Ceylon, a British Crown Colony, is an island in the Indian Ocean sixty miles off the southern tip of India. Ceylon has now attained the status of an independent nation within the British Commonwealth.

For later, independent coinage, see the listing under SRI LANKA, page 257.

CHAD (also TCHAD)

Coins		Current Worth
20,000 Francs	Gold	$1650
10,000 Francs	Gold	$ 750
5,000 Francs	Gold	$ 375
1,000 Francs	Gold	$ 75
300 Francs	Silver	$ 45
200 Francs	Silver	$ 30
100 Francs	Silver	$ 15
100 Francs	Nickel	$ 2.50

Higher values on silver and gold up to 20,000 Francs were issued in uncirculated condition.

A territory of French Equatorial Africa which became a republic in 1960.

Five Cents (Copper), 1870, worth $5

CHILE

Coins		Current Worth
100 Pesos	Gold	$400
50 Pesos	Gold	$250
20 Pesos	Gold	$150
10 Pesos	Gold	$125
5 Pesos	Gold	$100
5 Pesos	Silver	$ 27.50
2 Pesos	Silver	$ 13.50
1 Peso	Silver	$ 7.50
1 Peso	Copper-Nickel	50¢
50 Centavos	Silver	$ 7.50
40 Centavos	Silver	$ 4.50
20 Centavos	Silver	$ 1.75
10 Centavos	Silver	$ 1
5 Centavos	Silver	75¢
2 1/2 Centavos	Copper	$ 1.25
2 Centavos	Copper	$ 1.25
1 Centavo	Copper	75¢
Half Centavo	Copper	$ 1.25
1 Condor (10 Pesos)	Aluminum	$ 1.50
Half Condor	Aluminum	$ 1
1 Peso	Aluminum	35¢
1 Peso	Copper	50¢
50 Centavos	Copper	50¢
20 Centavos	Copper	20¢

New Valuation (1960–1975)

Coins		Current Worth
1971		
100 Escudos	Nickel-Brass	$ 1
50 Escudos	Nickel-Brass	65¢

CHILE (*cont.*)

Coins		Current Worth
10 Escudos	Aluminum	50¢
5 Escudos	Aluminum	25¢
5 Escudos	Copper-Nickel	75¢
1 Escudo	Copper-Nickel	35¢
50 Centesimos	Aluminum-Bronze	25¢
20 Centesimos	Aluminum-Bronze	20¢
10 Centesimos	Aluminum-Bronze	20¢
5 Centesimos	Aluminum-Bronze	15¢
2 Centesimos	Aluminum-Bronze	10¢
1 Centesimo	Aluminum	15¢
Half Centesimo	Aluminum	20¢

Reformed Coinage (1975 on)

Coins		Current Worth
1975		
10 Pesos	Copper-Nickel	$ 1
5 Pesos	Copper-Nickel	65¢
1 Peso	Copper-Nickel	50¢
50 Centavos	Copper-Nickel	35¢
10 Centavos	Aluminum	25¢
5 Centavos	Aluminum	20¢
1 Centavo	Aluminum	10¢

One Centavo (Copper), 1835, worth $2

The Republic of Chile lies on the west coast of South America, occupying the strip of land between the Andes and the South Pacific from Peru to Diego Ramirez Island. The mint of Santiago de Chile (Casa de Moneda), founded in 1743 by Philip V, King of Spain and Emperor of the West Indies, is one of the oldest established mints in America. Only the mints of Mexico, Potosi, Lima and Santa Fe de Nueva Granada were in operation before this.

20 Centavos (Copper-Nickel), 1922, worth $1

CHINA

Coins		Current Worth
20 Dollars	Gold	$800
10 Dollars	Gold	$475
1 Dollar	Silver	$ 25
50 Cents	Silver	$ 15
20 Cents	Silver	$ 5
10 Cents	Silver	$ 2.50
5 Cents	Nickel	75¢
5 Cents	Aluminum	30¢
1 Cent (10 Cash)	Aluminum	15¢

PEOPLE'S REPUBLIC

5 Cents	Aluminum	35¢
2 Cents	Aluminum	25¢
1 Cent (Fen)	Aluminum	20¢

Coins with denominations of $450, $400, $250 in gold, $20 silver, and $1 copper have been struck in proof form.

100 Cash (Copper), worth $5

7 Mace 2 Candereens (Silver), worth $35

Dollar (Silver), worth $100

Many varieties of Chinese provincial coins appeared during the Imperial regime, as well as the Republican period that followed. Coinage given above applies to the Republican era, with later evaluation (Chiao) as adopted by the Nationalist Government in Formosa.

China occupies the eastern part of Asia bounded on the north by Siberia, on the west by the Kazakh and Kirghiz Soviet Republics, on the southwest and south by the Himalayas from the Tibetan Indian frontier and French Indo-China, on the east by the China Sea and the Yellow Sea.

Formosa is the last stronghold of Nationalist China since 1950. It is an island between the Philippines on the south and Japan to the north, with the China Sea on the west and the Pacific Ocean on the east.

10 Cash (Copper), worth 60¢

COCOS (KEELING ISLANDS)

Coins		Current Worth
150 Rupees	Gold	$200
25 Rupees	Silver	$ 17.50
10 Rupees	Silver	$ 10
5 Rupees	Copper-Nickel	$ 5
2 Rupees	Copper-Nickel	$ 3.50
1 Rupee	Copper-Nickel	$ 2.50

COCOS (KEELING ISLANDS) (*cont.*)

Coins		Current Worth
50 Cents	Bronze	$ 1.25
25 Cents	Bronze	60¢
10 Cents	Bronze	40¢
5 Cents	Bronze	25¢

A group of small islands in the Indian Ocean now under the administration of Australia.

COLOMBIA

Coins		Current Worth
10 Pesos	Gold	$350
5 Pesos	Gold	$175
2 1/2 Pesos	Gold	$100
1 Peso	Silver	$ 25
50 Centavos	Silver	$ 12.50
20 Centavos	Silver	$ 6
10 Centavos	Silver	$ 3
5 Centavos	Silver	$ 2
5 Pesos	Copper-Nickel	$ 1.50
2 Pesos	Copper-Nickel	60¢
1 Peso	Copper-Nickel	75¢
50 Centavos	Copper-Nickel	75¢
20 Centavos	Copper-Nickel	50¢
10 Centavos	Copper-Nickel	25¢
5 Centavos	Copper-Nickel	75¢
5 Centavos	Bronze	20¢
2 Centavos	Copper-Nickel	75¢
2 Centavos	Aluminum-Nickel	20¢
1 Centavo	Copper-Nickel	35¢
1 Centavo	Bronze	15¢

Earlier coinages, prior to 1900, include 1/4, 1/2, 1 and 5 Decimo values (1 Decimo = 10 Centavos) as well as 1 1/4, 1 1/2 and 2 1/2 Centavos, ranging from $5 to $100 in current worth.

Recent Coinage

Coins		Current Worth
2 Pesos	Bronze	50¢
1 Peso	Copper-Nickel	20¢
50 Centavos	Steel-clad	15¢
20 Centavos	Aluminum-Brass	15¢
20 Centavos	Steel-clad	10¢
10 Centavos	Steel-clad	10¢
5 Centavos	Copper-clad	10¢
1 Centavo	Copper-clad	10¢

The Republic of Colombia is situated in the extreme northwest of South America and extends to the Republic of Panama. It has a coast line on the Pacific Ocean and on the Caribbean Sea. It touches Venezuela and Brazil on the east and Ecuador and Peru on the south.

Five Centavos (Nickel), worth $2

COMORO ISLANDS

Coins		Current Worth
100 Francs	Nickel	$ 2
50 Francs	Nickel	$ 1
20 Francs	Aluminum-Bronze	$ 1
10 Francs	Aluminum-Bronze	75¢
5 Francs	Aluminum-Bronze	60¢
2 Francs	Aluminum-Bronze	35¢
1 Franc	Aluminum-Bronze	25¢

This former French territory, now the independent Republic of the Comoros, is located in the Mozambique Channel between Africa and Madagascar.

CONGO
(See Zaire)

COOK ISLANDS

Coins		Current Worth
1 Dollar	Copper-Nickel	$ 7.50
50 Cents	Copper-Nickel	$ 1.50
20 Cents	Copper-Nickel	75¢
10 Cents	Copper-Nickel	35¢
5 Cents	Copper-Nickel	20¢
2 Cents	Bronze	15¢
1 Cent	Bronze	15¢

Gold and Silver commemorative coins have been issued in higher denominations and are available in uncirculated condition.

This territory of New Zealand was named in honor of the famous navigator, Captain James Cook. The coinage began in 1972.

COSTA RICA

Coins		Current Worth
20 Colones	Gold	$400
10 Colones	Gold	$200
5 Colones	Gold	$100
2 Colones	Gold	$ 75
50 Centimos	Silver	$ 25
10 Centimos	Silver	$ 4.50
5 Centimos	Silver	$ 2
2 Colones	Copper-Nickel	$ 1.50
1 Colon	Copper-Nickel	75¢
50 Centimos	Copper-Nickel	50¢
25 Centimos	Copper-Nickel	25¢
10 Centimos	Different Metals	15¢
5 Centimos	Different Metals	10¢

Recent Coinage (1970 on)

Coins		Current Worth
25 Colones	Silver	$ 65
20 Colones	Silver	$ 45
20 Colones	Nickel	$ 3.50
10 Colones	Silver	$ 25
10 Colones	Nickel	$ 2
5 Colones	Silver	$ 12.50
5 Colones	Nickel	$ 1
2 Colones	Silver	$ 5
2 Colones	Copper-Nickel	50¢
1 Colone	Copper-Nickel	25¢
50 Centimos	Copper-Nickel	20¢
20 Centimos	Copper-Nickel	20¢
10 Centimos	Copper-Nickel	15¢
5 Centimos	Copper-Nickel	10¢

The earlier units of Costa Rica currency (before 1900) were valued in gold pesos and silver centavos. Such coins are rarer than those listed under colones and centimos running up to twice their current worth. Gold coins of 5000, 1500, 500, 200, 100, and 50 colones have been struck as proofs. Also silver 300, 100, and 50.

Costa Rica, a republic in the southern part of Central America, touches Nicaragua on the north and Panama on the south.

Fifty Centavos (Silver), 1885, worth $15

CRETE

Coins		Current Worth
5 Drachmas	Silver	$ 35
2 Drachmas	Silver	$ 25
1 Drachma	Silver	$ 17.50
Half Drachma	Silver	$ 10
20 Lepta	Nickel	$ 3.50
10 Lepta	Nickel	$ 3.50
5 Lepta	Nickel	$ 3.50
2 Lepta	Copper	$ 4
1 Lepton	Copper	$ 4

Crete's coinage ceased after its union with Greece in 1908 and increased demand for coins of lower denominations (1 to 20 lepta) has raised the estimated worth of *very fine* specimens to the high figures quoted here.

CUBA

Coins		Current Worth
20 Pesos	Gold	$750
10 Pesos	Gold	$375
5 Pesos	Gold	$200
4 Pesos	Gold	$450
2 Pesos	Gold	$100
1 Peso	Gold	$250
1 Peso	Silver	$ 25
50 Centavos	Silver	$ 12.50
40 Centavos	Silver	$ 12.50
25 Centavos	Silver	$ 6.50
20 Centavos	Silver	$ 5
10 Centavos	Silver	$ 2.50
5 Centavos	Copper-Nickel	$ 1.25
2 Centavos	Copper-Nickel	$ 1
1 Centavo	Copper-Nickel	50¢

Five Centavos (Nickel), 1915, worth 60¢

CUBA
Castro Mintage

Coins		Current Worth
100 Pesos	Gold	$250
20 Pesos	Silver	$ 35
10 Pesos	Silver	$ 50

CUBA (*cont.*)

Coins		Current Worth
5 Pesos	Silver	$ 40
40 Centavos	Copper-Nickel	$ 2
20 Centavos	Copper-Nickel	$ 1
20 Centavos	Aluminum	$ 1
5 Centavos	Aluminum	15¢
1 Centavo	Aluminum	10¢

The Republic of Cuba is the largest island of the West Indies, lying among the Greater Antilles. The Gulf of Mexico and the Strait of Florida lie to the north, the Atlantic Ocean to the northeast, and the Caribbean Sea to the south.

One Peso (Silver), 1897, worth $75

CURACAO
(For Later Coinage See Netherlands Antilles)

Coins		Current Worth
2 1/2 Gulden	Silver	$ 25
1 Gulden (100 Cents)	Silver	$ 50
Quarter Gulden	Silver	$ 7
1/10 Gulden	Silver	$ 5
5 Cents (Diamond shaped)	Nickel	$ 7.50

CURACAO (*cont.*)

Coins		Current Worth
2 1/2 Cents	Copper	$ 2.50
1 Cent	Copper	$ 2

A Dutch island off the coast of Venezuela, Curacao is now a port of the Netherlands Antilles.

CYPRUS

Coins		Current Worth
45 Piastres	Silver	$ 10
19 Piastres	Silver	$ 2.50
9 Piastres	Silver	$ 1.50
4 1/2 Piastres	Silver	$ 1
3 Piastres	Silver	$ 1
1 Piastre	Copper-Nickel	$ 2
1 Piastre	Bronze	$ 1
Half Piastre	Copper-Nickel	$ 1.25
Half Piastre	Bronze	75¢
Quarter Piastre	Bronze	$ 12.50
2 Shillings	Copper-Nickel	$ 3
1 Shilling	Copper-Nickel	75¢

Cyprus is a republic and the third largest island in the Mediterranean Sea. Until 1960, it was a British Crown Colony.

CYPRUS
Decimal currency (1963 on)

Coins		Current Worth
50 Pounds	Gold	$350
1 Pound	Copper-Nickel	$ 3
500 Mils	Copper-Nickel	$ 1.50
100 Mils	Copper-Nickel	60¢

CYPRUS (*cont.*)

Coins		Current Worth
50 Mils	Copper-Nickel	30¢
25 Mils	Copper-Nickel	25¢
5 Mils	Bronze	15¢
1 Mil	Aluminum	10¢

CZECHOSLOVAKIA

Coins		Current Worth
20 Korona	Silver	$ 12.50
10 Korona	Silver	$ 7.50
5 Korona	Silver	$ 4.50
5 Korona	Copper-Nickel	$ 1.25
2 Korona	Copper-Nickel	50¢
1 Korona	Copper-Nickel	50¢
1 Korona	Aluminum	50¢
50 Haleru	Copper-Nickel or Aluminum	35¢
25 Haleru	Copper-Nickel or Aluminum	25¢
20 Haleru	Copper-Nickel or Aluminum	15¢
10 Haleru	Different Metals	15¢
5 Haleru	Different Metals	15¢
3 Haleru	Aluminum	15¢
2 Haleru	Zinc	$ 5
1 Haleru	Aluminum	10¢

Gold Commemorative Coins were minted in values of 1, 2, 4, 5 and 10 Ducats. Being limited in number and of interest to specialized collectors, these cannot be satisfactorily listed in terms of current worth. The same applies in lesser degree to silver commemorative coins which were minted in values of 10, 20, 25, 50 and 100 korona. These range from $10 to $50 in current worth, but are subject to fluctuations according to demand.

CZECHOSLOVAKIA (cont'd)
Additional values following Currency Reform (1953 on)

Coins		Current Worth
100 Korona	Silver	$ 10
50 Korona	Silver	$ 5
25 Korona	Silver	$ 7.50
10 Korona	Silver	$ 7.50
3 Korona	Copper-Nickel	50¢
1 Korona	Aluminum-Bronze	35¢
50 Haleru	Bronze	25¢

Czechoslovakia is a republic in Central Europe, a landlocked country without access to the sea. It is bounded on the north by Germany and Poland, on the south by Austria, Hungary and Ukrainian Soviet Socialist Republic, on the west by Germany, and on the east by Poland.

DANISH WEST INDIES
(Now U.S. Virgin Islands)

Coins		Current Worth
2 Francs (40 Cents)	Silver	$ 5
1 Franc (20 Cents)	Silver	$ 17.50
10 Cents	Silver	$ 7.50
5 Cents	Silver	$ 7.50
25 Bits (5 Cents)	Nickel	$ 5
10 Bits (2 Cents)	Copper-Bronze	$ 2.50
5 Bits (1 Cent)	Copper-Bronze	$ 2.50
2 1/2 Bits (Half Cent)	Copper-Bronze	$ 7.50

DENMARK

Coins		Current Worth
20 Kroner	Gold	$180
10 Kroner	Gold	$100
10 Kroner	Silver	$ 17.50
10 Kroner	Copper-Nickel	$ 2
5 Kroner	Silver	$ 15
5 Kroner	Copper-Nickel	$ 1
2 Kroner	Silver	$ 10
2 Kroner	Aluminum-Bronze	$ 1
1 Kroner	Silver	$ 7.50
1 Kroner	Aluminum-Bronze	$ 1
1 Kroner	Copper-Nickel	25¢
Half Kroner	Aluminum-Bronze	$ 5
25 Ore	Silver	$ 15
25 Ore	Copper-Nickel	25¢
25 Ore	Zinc	75¢
10 Ore	Silver	$ 5
10 Ore	Zinc	50¢
10 Ore	Copper-Nickel	15¢
5 Ore	Different Metals	15¢
2 Ore	Different Metals	15¢
1 Ore	Different Metals	10¢

The Kingdom of Denmark occupies the Peninsula of Jutland, north of Germany, between the North Sea and the Baltic Sea.

Ducat (Gold), 1775, worth $2500

Ducat (Gold), 1785, worth $350

Five Ore (Copper, later made of iron or zinc), 1874, worth $7.50

DJIBOUTI
Originally French Somaliland
Later known as Afars and Issas

Coins		Current Worth
100 Francs	Copper-Nickel	$ 7.50
50 Francs	Copper-Nickel	$ 5.50
*20 Francs	Aluminum-Bronze	$ 1
20 Francs	Aluminum-Bronze	75¢
*10 Francs	Aluminum-Bronze	75¢
10 Francs	Aluminum-Bronze	50¢
5 Francs	Aluminum	25¢
*5 Francs	Aluminum	50¢
2 Francs	Aluminum	10¢
*2 Francs	Aluminum	50¢
1 Franc	Aluminum	10¢
*1 Franc	Aluminum	50¢

*In 1948, it began issuing its own currency as indicated by the asterisks and in 1967 French Somaliland changed its name to Afars and Issas. A newer coinage followed (as given in the list and in 1977 the territory became an independent republic, named after its capital city, Djibouti.

DJIBOUTI *(cont.)*

A French Territory located between Ethiopia and Somalia on the straits that separate the Red Sea from the Gulf of Aden.

DOMINICAN REPUBLIC

Coins		Current Worth
1 Peso	Silver	$ 25
Half Peso	Silver	$ 12.50
25 Centavos	Silver	$ 6
20 Centavos	Silver	$ 3
10 Centavos	Silver	$ 2.50
10 Centavos	Copper-Nickel	30¢
5 Centavos	Silver	$ 14.50
5 Centavos	Copper-Nickel	15¢
1 Centavo	Bronze	15¢

The Dominican Republic occupies the eastern two thirds of the island of Hispaniola, second largest of the Greater Antilles, situated between Cuba on the west and Puerto Rico on the east.

Quarter Real (Brass), 1844, worth $5

One Centavo (Brass), 1877, worth $3.50

DOMINICAN REPUBLIC (*cont.*)

Recent Coinage (1920 on)

Coins		Current Worth
250 Pesos	Gold	$650
200 Pesos	Gold	$550
100 Pesos	Gold	$300
30 Pesos	Gold	$250
30 Pesos	Silver	$ 75
25 Pesos	Silver	$ 65
10 Pesos	Silver	$ 27.50
1 Peso	Copper-Nickel	$ 2.50
Half Peso	Copper-Nickel	$ 1.50
25 Pesos	Copper-Nickel	75¢
10 Pesos	Copper-Nickel	20¢
5 Pesos	Copper-Nickel	15¢
1 Peso	Bronze	10¢

Five Francs or One Peso (Silver) 1891, worth $50

EAST AFRICA

Coins		Current Worth
1 Shilling	Silver	$ 2.50
50 Cents (Half Shill)	Silver	$ 1.75
25 Cents	Silver	$ 5

EAST AFRICA (*cont.*)   Current
Coins   Worth

50 Cents	Copper-Nickel	75¢
10 Cents	Copper-Nickel	35¢
5 Cents	Bronze	$ 1
1 Cent	Bronze	50¢

A British colony formed by Kenya, Tanzania, and Uganda.

EAST CARIBBEAN TERRITORIES

Coins   Current
                                                     Worth

4 Dollars	Copper-Nickel	$ 5

These are minted in eight varieties bearing the individual titles of Antigua, Barbados, Dominica, Grenada, Montserrat, Saint Kitts, Saint Lucia, and Saint Vincent, all former members of the British Caribbean Territories. The old coinage is still in circulation throughout the islands named above.

ECUADOR

Coins   Current
                                                     Worth

1 Condor	Gold	$250
10 Sucres	Gold	$175
5 Sucres	Silver	$ 20
2 Sucres	Silver	$ 7.50
1 Sucre	Silver	$ 4.50
1 Sucre	Nickel	75¢
Half Sucre (50 Centavos)	Silver	$ 2.50
20 Centavos	Nickel or Brass	75¢
10 Centavos	Various Metals	50¢
5 Centavos	Various Metals	50¢
2 1/2 Centavos	Nickel	$ 2
2 Centavos	Copper-Nickel	$ 2.50
1 Centavo	Copper-Nickel	$ 3.50
1 Centavo	Bronze	60¢
Half Centavo	Copper-Nickel	$ 3.50

ECUADOR (*cont.*)

Coins		Current Worth
	Recent Coinage	
1 Sucre	Nickel-clad Steel	50¢
50 Centavos	Nickel-clad Steel	30¢
20 Centavos	Nickel-clad Steel	20¢
10 Centavos	Nickel-clad Steel	15¢
5 Centavos	Nickel-clad Steel	10¢

Ecuador on the Pacific Coast of South America extends from about 100 miles north of the Equator to 400 miles south of it. It is bounded by Colombia on the north and Peru on the east and south.

One Sucre (Silver), 1884, worth $25

EGYPT

Coins		Current Worth
500 Piastres	Gold	$950
100 Piastres	Gold	$200
50 Piastres	Gold	$125
20 Piastres	Gold	$ 60
20 Piastres	Silver	$ 25
10 Piastres	Silver	$ 12.50
5 Piastres	Silver	$ 6.50

EGYPT (*cont.*)

Coins		Current Worth
2 Piastres	Silver	$ 2.75
10 Milliemes	Copper-Nickel	60¢
5 Milliemes	Copper-Nickel	45¢
2 1/2 Milliemes (Octagonal)	Copper-Nickel	$ 1
2 Milliemes	Copper-Nickel	75¢
1 Millieme	Copper-Nickel	$ 1
1 Millieme	Bronze	35¢
Half Millieme	Bronze	60¢

(Recent Mintage)

10 Pounds	Gold	$950
5 Pounds	Gold	$500
1 Pound	Gold	$150
Half Pound	Gold	$ 85
1 Pound	Silver	$ 17.50
50 Piastres	Silver	$ 15
25 Piastres	Silver	$ 7.50
10 Piastres	Silver	$ 4.50
5 Piastres	Copper-Nickel	$ 1
20 Milliemes	Aluminum-Bronze	$ 1
10 Milliemes	Aluminum	75¢
10 Milliemes	Aluminum-Bronze	50¢
5 Milliemes	Aluminum	50¢
5 Milliemes	Aluminum-Bronze	25¢
2 Milliemes	Aluminum-Bronze	15¢
1 Millieme	Aluminum-Bronze	10¢

Egypt occupies the northeast corner of Africa with the Mediterranean Sea on the north and the Red Sea on the east. On the south is the Republic of the Sudan. Egypt now is sole member of the United Arab Republic, which included Syria from 1958 to 1961.

EL SALVADOR

Coins		Current Worth
20 Pesos	Gold	$2500
10 Pesos	Gold	$1500
5 Pesos	Gold	$ 950
2 1/2 Pesos	Gold	$ 650
1 Peso	Silver	$ 25
Half Peso	Silver	$ 12.50
Quarter Peso	Silver	$ 7.50
1/5 Peso	Silver	$ 17.50
1/10 Peso	Silver	$ 3.50
1/20 Peso	Silver	$ 2
5 Centavos	Copper-Nickel	75¢
3 Centavos	Copper-Nickel	$ 2
1 Centavo	Copper-Nickel	$ 1.25

Recent Coinage (1970 and later)

Coins		Current Worth
250 Colones (Pesos)	Gold	$350
25 Colones	Silver	$ 50
50 Centavos	Nickel	65¢
25 Centavos	Nickel	35¢
10 Centavos	Different Metals	25¢
5 Centavos	Different Metals	20¢
3 Centavos	Nickel-Brass	20¢
2 Centavos	Nickel-Brass	20¢
1 Centavo	Bronze	20¢
1 Centavo	Brass	15¢

Other silver and gold coins ranging from 1 colon to 200 colones have been struck in proof form only.

El Salvador, the smallest of the six Central American republics, and the only one without an Atlantic coastline, is bounded on the west by Guatemala; on the north and east by Honduras and the Gulf of Fonesca; and on the south by a Pacific coastline of about 160 miles.

One Peso (Silver), 1914, worth $25

EQUATORIAL AFRICAN STATES
(Now Central African States)

Coins		Current Worth
100 Francs	Nickel	$ 3.50
50 Francs	Copper-Nickel	$ 3
25 Francs	Aluminum-Bronze	75¢
10 Francs	Aluminum-Bronze	50¢
5 Francs	Aluminum-Bronze	35¢
1 Franc	Aluminum	20¢

EQUATORIAL AFRICAN STATES (*cont.*)

New Coinage (1975)

Coins		Current Worth
500 Francs	Copper-Nickel	$ 10
50 Francs	Nickel	$ 1.50
25 Francs	Aluminum-Bronze	$ 1
10 Francs	Aluminum-Bronze	60¢
5 Francs	Aluminum-Bronze	35¢
1 Franc	Aluminum-Bronze	15¢

Includes Cameroons, Chad, Central African Republic, Congo, and Gabon, as a monetary union.

EQUATORIAL GUINEA

Coins		Current Worth
50 Pesetas	Copper-Nickel	$ 4.50
25 Pesetas	Copper-Nickel	$ 2.50
5 Pesetas	Copper-Nickel	$ 1.50
1 Peseta	Aluminum-Bronze	75¢

New Coinage (1975)

10 Ekuele	Copper-Nickel	$ 1.50
5 Ekuele	Copper-Nickel	75¢
1 Ekuele	Copper-Nickel	35¢

Equatorial Guinea is a republic composed of the Island of Fernando Po off the west coast of Africa in the Bight of Biafra, an arm of the Gulf of Guinea. It includes a portion of the mainland facing the gulf.

ESTONIA

Coins		Current Worth
10 Marka	Nickel-Bronze	$ 10
*5 Marka	Nickel-Bronze	$ 7.50
*3 Marka	Nickel-Bronze	$ 6
*1 Marka	Nickel-Bronze	$ 5

*These are also struck in copper-nickel. They run about this same value if *extra fine* or better.

Later Currency

2 Krooni	Silver	$ 40
1 Krooni	Silver	$ 40
1 Krooni	Aluminum-Bronze	$ 12.50
50 Senti	Nickel-Bronze	$ 10
25 Senti	Nickel-Bronze	$ 7.50
20 Senti	Nickel-Bronze	$ 6
10 Senti	Nickel-Bronze	$ 5
5 Senti	Bronze	$ 3.50
2 Senti	Bronze	$ 3
1 Senti	Bronze	$ 2.50

Estonia, now a member of the U.S.S.R., is located on the eastern coast of the Baltic Sea. Its coinage, now obsolete, was issued between 1920 and 1940.

ETHIOPIA
(Abyssinia)

Coins		Current Worth
Dollar (Maria Theresa) (1780)	Silver	$ 25

ETHIOPIA (*cont.*)

Coins		Current Worth
Dollar (Menelik)	Silver	$ 25
Half Dollar (Menelik)	Silver	$ 12.50
Quarter Dollar (Menelik)	Silver	$ 6.50
2 Piastres (1/8 of $1)	Silver	$ 30
Piastre (1/16 of $1)	Silver	$ 3.50
Besa (1/2 Piastre)	Copper	$ 3
50 Cents (Haile Selassie)	Nickel	$ 2.50
25 Cents (Haile Selassie)	Nickel	$ 2
10 Cents (Haile Selassie)	Nickel	$ 1.25
5 Cents (Haile Selassie)	Copper	25¢
1 Cent (Haile Selassie)	Copper	15¢

Note: Maria Theresa Dollar is an old Austrian coin which continued to be struck bearing original date for circulation in Ethiopia and adjacent areas. Denominations of coins were changed following reign of Emperor Menelik to those of Haile Selassie.

Ethiopia, or Abyssinia, is a mountainous kingdom in northeast Africa, bounded by Eritrea, French Somaliland and British Somaliland on the northeast, Italian Somaliland on the southeast, Kenya Colony (British) on the south, and the Anglo-Egyptian Sudan on the west.

FIJI

Coins		Current Worth
Florin (2 Shillings)	Silver	$ 7.50
Florin	Copper-Nickel	$ 1.25
Shilling	Silver	$ 6
Shilling	Copper-Nickel	65¢
6 Pence	Silver	$ 3
6 Pence	Copper-Nickel	50¢
3 Pence	Nickel-Brass	30¢
1 Penny	Copper-Nickel	20¢
Half Penny	Copper-Nickel	10¢

Decimal Values (1969 on)

Coins		Current Worth
1 Dollar	Copper-Nickel	$ 5
50 Cents	Copper-Nickel	$ 2.50
20 Cents	Copper-Nickel	60¢
10 Cents	Copper-Nickel	30¢
5 Cents	Copper-Nickel	20¢
2 Cents	Bronze	10¢
1 Cent	Bronze	10¢

The Fiji Islands, more than 300 in number, form a British colony situated in the South Pacific, east of northern Australia. They became an independent democracy in 1970.

FINLAND

Coins		Current Worth
20 Markkaa	Gold	$ 200
10 Markkaa	Gold	$ 125
2 Markkaa	Silver	$ 25

FINLAND (*cont.*)

Coins		Current Worth
1 Markka	Silver	$ 7.50
50 Pennia	Silver	$ 3
25 Pennia	Silver	$ 2
10 Pennia	Copper	$ 1
5 Pennia	Copper	50¢
1 Penni	Copper	20¢

Above coins were types used under Imperial Russian rule prior to World War I (1914–1918). Following coins, with new currency valuation, are those of the Finnish Republic and bear later dates:

Coins		Current Worth
1000 Markkaa	Silver	$ 15
500 Markkaa	Silver	$ 20
200 Markkaa	Gold	$1200
200 Markkaa	Silver	$ 5
100 Markkaa	Gold	$1050
100 Markkaa	Silver	$ 3.50
50 Markkaa	Aluminum-Bronze	$ 2.50
25 Markkaa	Silver	$ 12.50
20 Markkaa	Aluminum-Bronze	$ 2
10 Markkaa	Aluminum-Bronze	75¢
5 Markkaa	Aluminum-Bronze	$ 1.50
5 Markkaa	Various Metals	50¢
1 Markka	Various Metals	50¢
50 Pennia	Various Metals	25¢
25 Pennia	Various Metals	20¢
10 Pennia	Various Metals	15¢
5 Pennia	Bronze	25¢

FINLAND (*cont.*)

Five Pennia (Copper), 1865–1875, worth $4

Reformed Currency (1962 on)

Coins		Current Worth
10 Markkaa	Silver	$ 15
10 Markkaa	Copper-Nickel	$ 1.50
1 Markka	Silver	$ 3
1 Markka	Copper-Nickel	50¢
50 Pennia	Aluminum-Bronze	35¢
20 Pennia	Aluminum-Bronze	20¢
10 Pennia	Aluminum-Bronze	15¢
5 Pennia	Aluminum-Bronze	10¢
1 Penni	Bronze or Aluminum	10¢

FRANCE

Coins		Current Worth
100 Francs	Gold	$650
20 Francs	Gold	$135
10 Francs	Gold	$ 65
5 Francs	Silver	$ 12
2 Francs	Silver	$ 10
1 Franc	Silver	$ 5

FRANCE (*cont.*)

Coins		Current Worth
50 Centimes	Silver	$ 2.50
25 Centimes	Nickel	75¢
10 Centimes	Various Metals	15¢
5 Centimes	Various Metals	15¢
2 Centimes	Copper	15¢
1 Centime	Copper	10¢
(A)*20 Francs	Silver	$ 15
10 Francs	Silver	$ 7.50
10 Francs	Copper-Nickel	$ 1
5 Francs	Nickel	$ 2
5 Francs	Aluminum	50¢
2 Francs	Aluminum	20¢
1 Franc	Aluminum	10¢
50 Centimes	Aluminum	10¢
25 Centimes	Copper-Nickel	20¢
10 Centimes	Copper-Nickel	10¢
5 Centimes	Copper-Nickel	25¢
2 Centimes	Copper-Nickel	10¢
(B) *50 Francs	Aluminum-Bronze	75¢
20 Francs	Aluminum-Bronze	40¢
10 Francs	Aluminum-Bronze	20¢

New Coinage (1960 on)

50 Francs	Silver	$ 35
10 Francs	Silver	$ 25
10 Francs	Nickel-Brass	$ 3
5 Francs	Silver	$ 12.50
5 Francs	Nickel-clad-Copper	$ 2
2 Francs	Nickel	$ 1
1 Franc	Nickel	50¢
Half Franc	Nickel	35¢

FRANCE (*cont.*)

Coins		Current Worth
50 Centimes	Aluminum-Bronze	35¢
20 Centimes	Aluminum-Bronze	20¢
10 Centimes	Aluminum-Bronze	15¢
5 Centimes	Aluminum-Bronze	10¢
5 Centimes	Chrome-Steel	10¢
1 Centimes	Chrome-Steel	10¢

Note: Coins beginning with "A" were issued following World War I, bearing dates after 1920. Those beginning with "B" were issued following World War II, with dates after 1950.

Louis XIII Ecu (Silver, 1704, worth $200 Rare

Louis XIV Ecu (Silver), 1758, worth $150 Rare

Reformed Currency (1959 on)

Coins		Current Worth
50 Francs	Silver	$ 35
10 Francs	Silver	$ 25
10 Francs	Nickel-Brass	$ 3
5 Francs	Silver	$ 12.50
5 Francs	Nickel-clad Copper	$ 2
1 Franc	Nickel	40¢
Half Franc	Nickel	35¢
50 Centimes	Aluminum-Bronze	35¢
20 Centimes	Aluminum-Bronze	20¢
10 Centimes	Aluminum-Bronze	15¢
5 Centimes	Aluminum-Bronze	10¢
5 Centimes	Chrome-Steel	10¢
1 Centime	Chrome-Steel	10¢

The Republic of France is the most westerly country of Central Europe. On the east and northeast lie Belgium and Luxemburg, with Germany across the Rhine River. The Jura Mountains and Lake Geneva separate it from Switzerland, and the Alps separate it

from Italy on the southeast. On the south are the Mediterranean
Sea and the Pyrenees separating it from Spain. On the west are Bay
of Biscay and the Atlantic Ocean, and on the north is the English
Channel and the Straits of Dover, separating it from England.

Francis I Ecu (Gold), about 1515, worth $40

Louis XV (Gold Louis), 1719, worth $25

Louis XVI (Gold Louis), 1774, worth $350

Forty Francs of Napoleon (Gold), 1805, worth $350

Twenty Francs of Napoleon (Gold), 1805, worth $150

One Decime (Copper), 1798, worth $40

Ten Centimes (Copper), 1855, worth $2.50

FRENCH EQUATORIAL AFRICA

Coins		Current Worth
25 Francs	Aluminum-Bronze	$ 1.50
10 Francs	Aluminum-Bronze	85¢
5 Francs	Aluminum-Bronze	65¢
2 Francs	Aluminum	35¢
1 Franc	Aluminum	20¢
1 Franc	Bronze	$ 1.50
1 Franc	Brass	$ 1.50
50 Centimes	Bronze	$ 1.25
50 Centimes	Brass	$ 1.25

A group of former French Colonies, with coins inscribed AFRIQUE EQUITORIALE FRANCAISE, which have been superseded by the Equatorial African States, with coinage listed under that head.

FRENCH INDO CHINA

Coins		Current Worth
1 Piastre	Copper-Nickel	$ 10
50 Centimes	Copper-Nickel	$ 1.50
20 Centimes	Aluminum	20¢
20 Centimes	Nickel	$ 10.00
20 Centimes	Copper-Nickel	20¢

FRENCH INDO CHINA (*cont.*)

Coins		Current Worth
10 Centimes	Nickel	25¢
10 Centimes	Copper-Nickel	20¢
10 Centimes	Aluminum	35¢
5 Centimes	Aluminum	10¢
5 Centimes	Copper-Nickel	75¢
5 Centimes	Nickel-Brass	35¢
1 Centime	Aluminum	25¢
1 Centime	Zinc	$ 1.25
1 Centime	Bronze	75¢
Half Centime	Bronze	25¢
Quarter Centime	Zinc	$ 7.50

A territory consisting of the present states of Cambodia, Laos, North Vietnam and South Vietnam, which ceased to be under French jurisdiction in 1953, all coinage being prior to that date.

FRENCH POLYNESIA
(Formerly French Oceania)

Coins		Current Worth
100 Francs	Nickel-Bronze	$ 2.50
50 Francs	Nickel	$ 1.75
20 Francs	Nickel	$ 1
10 Francs	Nickel	75¢
5 Francs*	Aluminum	50¢
2 Francs*	Aluminum	35¢
1 Franc*	Aluminum	20¢
50 Centimes*	Aluminum	35¢

Includes the Society Islands and five other groups in the South Pacific Ocean, with the capital at Papeete on the Island of Tahiti.

*These are stamped OCEANIE prior to 1965; POLYNESIE from then on.

FRENCH WEST AFRICA

Coins		Current Worth
25 Francs	Aluminum-Bronze	$ 1.50
10 Francs	Aluminum-Bronze	75¢
5 Francs	Aluminum-Bronze	35¢
2 Francs	Aluminum	25¢
1 Franc	Aluminum	20¢
1 Franc	Aluminum-Bronze	$ 1.50
50 Centimes	Aluminum-Bronze	$ 1.25

Coinage integrated with *Togo*:

25 Francs	Aluminum-Bronze	50¢
10 Francs	Aluminum-Bronze	25¢

For coinage later than 1958 and description of this territory, see *West African States.*

GABON

Coins		Current Worth
100 Francs	Nickel	$ 2.50
25 Francs	Gold	$175
10 Francs	Gold	$100

Proofs have been struck of gold coins in denominations of 50, 100, 1,000, 3,000, 5,000, and 20,000 francs but so far none have been recognized as regular coinage. It is an independent republic formerly a territory of French Equatorial Africa.

THE REPUBLIC OF GAMBIA

Coins		Current Worth
8 Shillings	Silver	$ 60
8 Shillings	Copper-Nickel	$ 5
4 Shillings	Copper-Nickel	$ 2.50
2 Shillings	Copper-Nickel	75¢
1 Shilling	Copper-Nickel	50¢
6 Pence	Copper-Nickel	25¢
3 Pence	Nickel-Brass	20¢
1 Penny	Bronze	15¢

New Decimal Values (Beginning 1971)

Coins		Current Worth
500 Dalasis	Gold	$750
40 Dalasis	Silver	$ 50
20 Dalasis	Silver	$ 35
10 Dalasis	Silver	$ 15
1 Dalasi	Copper-Nickel	$ 1.50
50 Bututs	Copper-Nickel	$ 1
25 Bututs	Copper-Nickel	60¢
10 Bututs	Nickel-Brass	30¢
10 Bututs	Bronze	30¢
5 Bututs	Bronze	20¢
1 Butut	Bronze	10¢

The Republic of Gambia is a former British Colony near the extreme western bulge of Africa and represents the continent's smallest nation.

GERMANY
Before World War I

Coins		Current Worth
20 Marks	Gold	$150
10 Marks	Gold	$ 75
5 Marks	Silver	$ 30
3 Marks	Silver	$ 15
2 Marks	Silver	$ 10
1 Mark	Silver	$ 5
50 Pfennig (Half Mark)	Silver	$ 2.50
25 Pfennig	Nickel	$ 2
20 Pfennig	Silver	$ 3
10 Pfennig	Copper-Nickel	25¢
5 Pfennig	Copper-Nickel	25¢
2 Pfennig	Copper	20¢
1 Pfennig	Copper	10¢

EAST GERMANY
(German Democratic Republic)

Coins		Current Worth
20 Marks	Silver	$ 15
20 Marks	Copper-Nickel	$ 3.50
10 Marks	Silver	$ 10
10 Marks	Copper-Nickel	$ 5
5 Marks	Copper-Nickel	$ 2.50
2 Marks	Aluminum	$ 1.25
1 Mark	Aluminum	75¢
50 Pfennig	Aluminum	40¢
20 Pfennig	Aluminum	25¢
10 Pfennig	Aluminum	25¢
5 Pfennig	Aluminum	25¢
1 Pfennig	Aluminum	15¢

WEST GERMANY

(Bundes Republik, Federal Republic)

Coins		Current Worth
5 Marks	Silver	$ 7.50
2 Marks	Copper-Nickel	$ 1.50
1 Mark	Copper-Nickel	75¢
50 Pfennig	Copper-Nickel	35¢
10 Pfennig	Steel	20¢
5 Pfennig	Steel	15¢
2 Pfennig	Steel	10¢
1 Pfennig	Steel	10¢

Germany in Central Europe is bounded on the north by the North Sea, the Baltic Sea and Denmark; on the east by Poland, Czechoslovakia, and Austria; on the south by Austria and Switzerland; on the west by France, Luxemburg, Belgium, the Netherlands and the North Sea.

Buchenwald Concentration Camp Money (Paper). 1939, worth $1

Three Pfennig (Copper) 1871, worth $1.50
Prussia

Two Pfennig (Copper), 1874, worth $2

Prussia Frederick D'or (Gold), 1796, worth $400

Bavaria Ducat (Gold), 1801, worth $1,250

Saxony Ducat (Gold), 1772, worth $750

Hamburg Ducat (Gold), 1781, worth $250

Mecklenburg Eight Groschen (Silver), 1754, worth $25

Wurtemburg One Sixth Reichs Thaler (Silver), 1758, worth $12

Brunswick Luneberg Eight Groschen (Silver), 1759, worth $25

Prussia One Third Reichs Thaler (Silver), 1759, worth $25

Wurtemburg 1/6 Thaler (Silver), 1758, worth $12

Twenty Krenzh Chur Pfalz (Silver), 1735, worth $15

GHANA

Coins		Current Worth
2 Shillings	Copper-Nickel	$ 1.50
1 Shilling	Copper-Nickel	50¢
6 Pence	Copper-Nickel	30¢
3 Pence	Copper-Nickel	25¢
1 Penny	Bronze	20¢
Half Penny	Bronze	10¢

New Monetary System
(Beginning in 1965)

Coins		Current Worth
50 Pesewas	Copper-Nickel	$ 1.50
25 Pesewas	Copper-Nickel	$ 1
20 Pesewas	Copper-Nickel	$ 1
10 Pesewas	Copper-Nickel	50¢
5 Pesewas	Copper-Nickel	25¢
2 1/2 Pesewas	Copper-Nickel	25¢
1 Pesewa	Bronze	15¢
Half Pesewa	Bronze	10¢

Ghana is a republic composed of the former British Colony of Gold Coast, including outlying territories. It is situated on the Gulf of Guinea in West Africa, bounded on the north by Mali and Upper Volta, on the east by Togoland, on the west by the Ivory Coast and on the south by the Atlantic Ocean.

GIBRALTAR

Coins		Current Worth
1 Crown	Silver	$ 60
1 Crown	Copper-Nickel	$ 3
25 New Pence	Silver	$ 40
25 New Pence	Copper-Nickel	$ 2

British coins are used for lesser values.

Gilbraltar is a British Colony off the southern tip of Spain. It consists of a towering rock guarding the entrance to the Mediterranean Sea and its harbor is also used as a naval base.

GREAT BRITAIN

Coins		Current Worth
Sovereign	Gold	$175
Half Sovereign	Gold	$ 95
5 Shillings (Crown)	Silver	$ 27.50
5 Shillings	Copper-Nickel	$ 4.50
Half Crown	Silver	$ 10
2 1/2 Shillings	Copper-Nickel	$ 1.25
2 Shillings (Florin)	Silver	$ 7.50
2 Shillings	Copper-Nickel	$ 1
1 Shilling	Silver	$ 1.50
1 Shilling	Copper-Nickel	25¢

GREAT BRITAIN (*cont.*)

Coins		Current Worth
6 Pence	Silver	$ 1.75
6 Pence	Copper-Nickel	20¢
3 Pence	Silver	75¢
3 Pence	Copper-Nickel	35¢
1 Penny	Copper	35¢
Halfpenny	Copper	35¢
Quarter Penny (Farthing)	Copper	35¢

Great Britain is an island kingdom of northwest Europe composed of England, Wales, Scotland and Northern Ireland.

Channel Islands (Silver), 700-900 A.D., worth $3.50

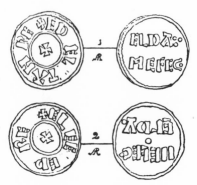

Anglo Saxon (Silver), 700-900 A.D., worth $400

Guinea of Queen Anne (Gold), 1713, worth $350

Rose Guinea of George III (Gold), 1784, worth $200

Spade Guinea of George III (Gold), 1790, worth $200

Half Guinea of George III (Gold), 1787, worth $175

Farthing (Copper), 1721, worth $10

Halfpenny (Copper), 1887, worth $1.50

One Penny (Copper), about 1893, worth $1

The *pennies* of Kings William I, William II, Henry I, and Stephen bear titles, profile or fullfaced bust on Obverse; and on the Reverse they bear variously shaped and ornamental crosses, surrounded by the moneyer's name and the place of mintage.

The *pennies* of Henry II and Henry III bear the king's title and full face on Obverse; and on the Reverse there is a long or short double cross extending to the edge of the coin, with three pellets in each angle, within an inner beaded circle, surrounded by the moneyer's name and the place of mintage.

The *pennies* of Edwards I, II, III and IV, and the *pennies* of Henrys V and VI bear the titles and fullfaced bust, crowned, on the Obverse; while on the Reverse is shown a long single cross extending to the edge of the coin, three pellets in each angle, surrounded by the name of the mint, preceded by the word VILLA (town) or CIVITAS (city), thus: CIVITAS CANTOR (Canterbury); VILLA CALISIE (Calais). Halfpennies and farthings are similar.

Groats of Edwards III, IV and V and of Henrys IV, V, VI and VII (first and second issues) bear on the Obverse the full-faced bust, crowned, within a treasure of nine arches. On the Reverse there is a long cross extending to the edge of the coin, three pellets in each angle of the cross, surrounded by two circles. In the inner circle the name of the town where coined is given, as on the pennies. In the outer circle there is the motto POSVI: DEVM: ADIVTOREM: MEVM, with various mint marks. *Half groats* are similar.

Groats with the portrait of Henry VII (the first authentic portrait on English coins) bear profile bust of the king crowned. On the Reverse there is a large shield of arms and over it a long cross with forked ends, with an outer circle showing the motto POSVI: DEVM: ADIVTOREM: MEVM. The groats from this period bear profile or full-faced bust of the king or queen crowned. On the Reverse there is a large shield of arms with mottoes and mint marks.

Sixpences (hammered) from Edward VI to Charles I have the bust of the king or queen, full face or profile to left or right, as described in each reign. On the Reverse there is a large shield variously shaped, with the arms of England and France, and these arms are quartered from Edward III to Elizabeth I's reign. Coins from the time of James I and Charles I bear the arms of England and France in first and fourth quarters, the arms of Scotland and Ireland in second and third quarters.

Shillings (hammered) from Edward VI, James I, and Charles I have on the Obverse the king on horseback. On the Reverse are shown variously shaped shield of arms, according to reign and place of mintage, and different mint marks. The early *half crown* (hammered) comes in similar varieties.

Crowns (milled), from Charles II to George II, have on the Obverse profile bust of the king or queen, to right or left. On the Reverse there are four shields crowned. In the angles of most issues there are various letters, plumes, roses and plumes, etc. The shields usually bear English, French, Scottish or Irish arms. *Half-crowns* (milled) are in similar varieties.

GREAT BRITAIN (*cont.*)

Decimal Values (1968 on)

Coins		Current Worth
1 Pound	Nickel-Brass	$ 5.00
50 New Pence	Copper-Nickel	$ 2.00
20 New Pence	Copper-Nickel	$ 1.00
10 New Pence	Copper-Nickel	50¢
5 New Pence	Copper-Nickel	30¢
2 New Pence	Bronze	15¢
1 New Penny	Bronze	10¢
Half New Penny	Bronze	10¢

GREECE

Coins		Current Worth
20 Drachmae	Gold	$250
5 Drachmae	Silver	$ 45
2 Drachmae	Silver	$ 12.50
1 Drachma	Silver	$ 5
50 Lepta	Silver	15¢
20 Lepta	Nickel	50¢
10 Lepta	Nickel	40¢
10 Lepta	Copper	$ 1
5 Lepta	Copper	75¢
5 Lepta	Nickel	35¢
20 Drachmae	Silver	$ 8.50
10 Drachmae	Silver	$ 5
5 Drachmae	Copper-Nickel	75¢
2 Drachmae	Copper-Nickel	35¢
1 Drachmae	Copper-Nickel	30¢

Later Coinage

Coins		Current Worth
50 Lepta	Nickel	25¢
20 Lepta	Aluminum	20¢
10 Lepta	Aluminum	10¢

Ten Lepta (Copper), 1837, worth $12.50

Five Drachmae (Silver), worth $100

New Coinage (Republic 1973)

Coins		Current Worth
20 Drachmae	Copper-Nickel	$ 3
10 Drachmae	Copper-Nickel	$ 1.50
5 Drachmae	Copper-Nickel	$ 1
2 Drachmae	Nickel-Copper	50¢
1 Drachma	Nickel-Copper	35¢
50 Lepta	Nickel-Copper	25¢
20 Lepta	Aluminum	15¢
10 Lepta	Aluminum	10¢

Greece occupies the southern peninsula of the Balkans, in the Meditteranean Sea, with the Ionian Sea on the west and the Aegean Sea on the east. On the northwest lies Albania, on the north Yugoslavia and Bulgaria, and on the northeast Turkey.

GREENLAND

Coins		Current Worth
5 Kroner	Brass	$ 17.50
1 Krone	Aluminum-Bronze	$ 3.50
1 Krone	Copper-Nickel	$ 2.50
50 Ore	Aluminum-Bronze	$ 1.50
25 Ore	Copper-Nickel	$ 1.50

The world's largest island surrounded by the Atlantic and Arctic Oceans, belongs to Denmark.

GUATEMALA

Coins		Current Worth
1 Peso	Silver	$ 30
50 Centavos	Silver	$ 10
25 Centavos	Silver	$ 5
25 Centavos	Copper	$ 1.50
12 1/2 Centavos	Copper	$ 1.50
4 Reales	Silver	$ 15
2 Reales	Silver	$ 8.50
1 Real	Silver	$ 3.50
Half Real	Silver	$ 2.50
5 Pesos	Aluminum	$ 4
1 Peso	Aluminum	$ 1.75
50 Centavos	Aluminum	$ 1.50
2 Centavos	Copper	20¢
1 Centavo	Copper	10¢
Half Quetzal	Silver	$ 37.50
Quarter Quetzal	Silver	$ 10

GUATEMALA (*cont.*)

New Coinage (1965 on)

Coins		Current Worth
25 Centavos	Nickel-Brass	$ 1
10 Centavos	Nickel-Brass	40¢
5 Centavos	Nickel-Brass	75¢
1 Centavo	Brass	15¢

The Republic of Guatemala, the most northerly state of Central America, touches Mexico on the north and west, British Honduras on the east, Honduras and Salvador on the east and south, and the Pacific Ocean on the southwest.

Eight Reales or Pesos (Silver), 1824, worth $50

Pesos (Silver), 1894, worth $25

Peso (Silver), 1871, worth $25

Fifty Centavos (Silver), 1870 worth $25

GUERNSEY
(See also Jersey)

Coins		Current Worth
8 Double Piece	Copper	$ 2
4 Double Piece	Copper	$ 1.50
2 Double Piece	Copper	$ 1.50
1 Double Piece	Copper	$ 1.25
10 Shillings	Copper-Nickel (1966)	$ 3.50
3 Pence	Copper-Nickel	75¢

GUERNSEY (*cont.*)

Coins		Current Worth
	Decimal Values (1968 on)	
1 Pound	Copper-Nickel-Zinc	$ 4
50 New Pence	Copper-Nickel	$ 1.50
25 New Pence	Copper-Nickel	$ 1.25
10 New Pence	Copper-Nickel	35¢
5 New Pence	Copper-Nickel	25¢
2 New Pence	Bronze	15¢
1 New Penny	Bronze	10¢

These pieces represent the only local coinage, but in addition to these British sterling, as well as French gold and silver coins, circulate on the Island of Guernsey.

The Channel Islands off the northwest coast of France are the only portions of the Dukedom of Normandy belonging to England, to which country they have been attached since the Norman conquest. The islands consist of Jersey, Guernsey and the dependencies of Guernsey.

Four Doubles (Copper), 1830, worth $7.50

GUINEA

Coins		Current Worth
25 Frances	Aluminum-Bronze	$ 8
25 Francs	Copper-Nickel	$ 1.50
10 Francs	Aluminum-Bronze	$ 1.25
10 Francs	Copper-Nickel	75¢
5 Francs	Aluminum-Bronze	$ 1
5 Francs	Copper-Nickel	50¢
1 Franc	Copper-Nickel	25¢

New Coinage

5 Sylis	Aluminum	$ 2.50
2 Sylis	Aluminum	$ 1.50
1 Syli	Aluminum	$ 1.25
50 Cauris	Aluminum	$ 1

The Republic of Guinea is a former French Overseas Territory, located on the west coast of Africa and bonded by Portuguese Guinea and Senegal on the north; by Mali on the northeast; by Ivory Coast on the southeast; and Sierra Leone and Liberia on the south.

GUYANA

Coins		Current Worth
1 Dollar	Copper-Nickel	$ 2
50 Cents	Copper-Nickel	$ 1
25 Cents	Copper-Nickel	60¢
10 Cents	Copper-Nickel	30¢
5 Cents	Nickel-Brass	20¢
1 Cent	Nickel-Brass	20¢

The Republic of Guyana consists of the former British Colony of British Guiana, becoming independent in 1966. Situated on the northeast coast of South America, Guiana is bounded on the west by Venezuela; on the west and south by Brazil; and on the east by Surinam.

HAITI

Coins		Current Worth
Gourde	Silver	$ 30
50 Centimes	Silver	$ 12.50
20 Centimes	Silver	$ 4.50
10 Centimes	Silver	$ 2
2 Centimes	Copper	$ 3
1 Centime	Copper	$ 2.50
50 Cents	Copper-Nickel	75¢
20 Cents	Copper-Nickel	50¢
10 Cents	Copper-Nickel	30¢
5 Cents	Copper-Nickel	20¢

The Republic of Haiti occupies the western third of the island known as Hispaniola, the second largest of the Greater Antilles, lying between Cuba on the west and Puerto Rico on the east.

One Gourde (Silver), 1881, worth $35

100 Centimes (Silver), 1832-1833, Years 26-27
after the Liberation, worth $25

Six Centimes (Copper), 1846, worth $7.50

Fifty Centimes (Nickel), 1908, worth $2

HONDURAS

Coins		Current Worth
1 Peso (100 Centavos)	Silver	$ 35
Half Peso (50 Centavos)	Silver	$ 15
Quarter Peso (25 Centavos)	Silver	$ 7.50
10 Centavos	Silver	$ 10
5 Centavos	Silver	$ 5
2 Centavos	Bronze	$ 2.50
1 Centavo	Bronze	$ 2
Half Centavo	Bronze	$ 15
	New Coinage	
1 Lempira	Silver	$ 12.50
50 Centavos (Half Lempira)	Silver	$ 6
20 Centavos	Silver	$ 2.50
10 Centavos	Copper-Nickel	30¢
5 Centavos	Copper-Nickel	15¢
2 Centavos	Bronze or Steel	10¢
1 Centavo	Bronze or Steel	10¢

The republic of Honduras is in Central America, bounded on the north by the Caribbean Sea, on the east and south by Nicaragua, on the south and west by Salvador, and on the west by Guatemala.

Eight Pesos (Copper), 1862, worth $25

HONG KONG

Coins		Current Worth
5 Dollars (British)	Copper-Nickel	$ 2
2 Dollars (British)	Copper-Nickel	75¢
1 Dollar (British)	Silver	$ 65
50 Cents (British)	Silver	$ 20
20 Cents (British)	Silver	$ 10
10 Cents (British)	Silver	$ 2.50
5 Cents (British)	Silver	$ 1
1 Cent	Copper	25¢
5 Dollars	Copper-Nickel	$ 1.50
2 Dollars	Copper-Nickel	75¢
1 Dollar	Copper-Nickel	50¢
50 Cents	Copper-Nickel	75¢
20 Centavos	Nickel-Brass	15¢
10 Cents	Nickel	25¢
5 Cents	Nickel	10¢

Hong Kong is a British Crown Colony (acquired in 1841) which lies at the mouth of the Canton River, China.

One Cent (Copper), 1875, worth $2

HUNGARY

Coins		Current Worth
100 Kronen	Gold	$750
20 Kronen	Gold	$150
10 Kronen	Gold	$ 75
5 Kronen	Silver	$ 22.50
2 Kronen	Silver	$ 8.50
1 Krone	Silver	$ 4.50
20 Filler	Nickel	$ 1
10 Filler	Nickel	50¢
2 Filler	Bronze	25¢
1 Filler	Bronze	25¢

Coinage After World War I

5 Pengo	Silver	$ 20
2 Pengo	Silver	$ 7.50
1 Pengo	Silver	$ 3.50
5 Pengo	Aluminum	$ 2.50
2 Pengo	Aluminum	75¢
1 Pengo	Aluminum	35¢

Coinage After World War II

10 Forint	Silver	$ 12.50
5 Forint	Silver	$ 7.50
2 Forint	Nickel or Aluminum	75¢
1 Forint	Aluminum	75¢
50 Filler	Aluminum	50¢
20 Filler	Aluminum	30¢
10 Filler	Aluminum	15¢
5 Filler	Aluminum	10¢
2 Filler	Aluminum	10¢

The Republic of Hungary in Central Europe is bounded by Czechoslovakia and the Union of Soviet Socialist Republics on the north, by Yugoslavia on the south, by Rumania on the east, and by Austria on the west.

Ducat (Gold), 1750, worth $250

One Florin (Silver), 1869, worth $15

Five Pengo (Silver), 1939, worth $20

ICELAND

Coins		Current Worth
10,000 Kronur	Gold	$300
1,000 Kronur	Gold	$ 35
500 Kronur	Gold	$275
500 Kronur	Silver	$ 20
50 Kronur	Nickel	$ 1.50
50 Kronur	Copper-Nickel	$ 1.25
10 Kronur	Copper-Nickel	75¢
5 Kronur	Copper-Nickel	50¢
2 Kronur	Nickel or Aluminum	$ 1
1 Krona	Nickel or Aluminum	60¢
25 Aurar	Copper-Nickel	35¢
10 Aurar	Copper-Nickel	25¢
5 Aurar	Copper-Bronze	15¢
1 Eyrir	Copper-Bronze	15¢

Later Dates

50 Aurar	Nickel-Brass	15¢
10 Aurar	Aluminum	10¢
5 Aurar	Bronze	10¢

The Republic of Iceland is an island in the North Atlantic close to the Arctic Circle. It is of volcanic origin and has many geysers and hot springs. Iceland was formerly a dependency of Denmark.

INDIA
British Coinage

Coins		Current Worth
Mohur (15 Rupees)	Gold	$350
Rupee	Silver	$ 7.50
Rupee	Nickel	$ 1.50
Half Rupee (8 Annas)	Silver	$ 3.50
Half Rupee (8 Annas)	Nickel	50¢
Quarter Rupee (4 Annas)	Silver	$ 1.75
Quarter Rupee (4 Annas)	Nickel	30¢
1 Anna	Copper-Nickel	15¢
Half Anna	Copper-Nickel	15¢
1 Pice (Quarter Anna)	Copper	15¢
Half Pice	Copper	15¢

Many coins of these and other denominations have been issued by various Native States and some are classed as rare collector's items.

Coins		Current Worth
	Republic Coinage	
Rupee	Nickel	75¢
50 Naya Paise (Half Rupee)	Nickel	75¢
25 Naya Paise	Nickel	40¢
10 Naya Paise	Copper-Nickel	25¢
5 Naya Paise	Copper-Nickel	15¢
2 Naya Paise	Copper-Nickel	10¢
1 Naya Paise	Bronze	10¢

INDIA (*cont.*)

Coins		Current Worth
	Decimal Coinage	
20 Rupees	Silver	$ 25
10 Rupees	Silver	$ 12.50
10 Rupees	Copper-Nickel	$ 3
50 Paise	Copper-Nickel	50¢
25 Paise	Copper-Nickel	30¢
20 Paise	Aluminum-Bronze	20¢
10 Paise	Various Metals	15¢
5 Paise	Aluminum	10¢
3 Paise	Aluminum	10¢
2 Paise	Aluminum	10¢
2 Paise	Copper-Nickel	15¢
1 Paisa	Aluminum	10¢
1 Paisa	Nickel-Brass	15¢

The new Republic of India embraces the larger geographical and population division of the subcontinent of India. It consists of the predominantly Hindu provinces and the vast majority of the 562 former independent princely native states: Bombay, Madras, Uttar, Pradesh, Madhya Pradesh, Bihar, Orissa, the eastern half of Punjab, the western half of Bengal Delhi, Ajmer and Coorg.

The Dominion of India, raised to British dominion status along with Pakistan on August 15, 1947, became a sovereign democratic republic under a constitution adopted November 26, 1949, effective January 26, 1950. It elected to remain a member of the Commonwealth of Nations, the name "British" being omitted.

The Dominion of Pakistan, one of the largest countries in the world, comprises two zones in the northeast and northwest corners of the Indo-Pakistan subcontinent, separated by a thousand miles of territory of the Republic of India. Pakistan was formed by the partition of the subcontinent of India on August 15, 1947, on the basis of Islamic faith of the majority of the population.

Mohur (Gold), 1862, worth $250

INDONESIA

Coins		Current Worth
50 Sen	Copper-Nickel or Aluminum	$ 1
25 Sen	Aluminum	60¢
10 Sen	Aluminum	30¢
5 Sen	Aluminum	25¢
1 Sen	Aluminum	20¢

The Republic of Indonesia lies along the Equator between the Asiatic mainland and the Philippine Islands and Australia.

Above prices apply to similar aluminum coinage of West Indonesia and the Rial Archipelago, which are now obsolete and therefore subject to rapid fluctuation.

INDONESIA (*cont.*)

Coins		Current Worth
	Later Coinage	
100 Rupiah	Copper-Nickel	$ 1.50
50 Rupiah	Copper-Nickel	90¢
25 Rupiah	Copper-Nickel	50¢
10 Rupiah	Various Metals	20¢
5 Rupiah	Aluminum	20¢
2 Rupiah	Aluminum	15¢
1 Rupiah	Aluminum	10¢

Coinage ranging from 200 Rupiah (silver) to 100,000 Rupiah (gold) have been struck chiefly in proof form so are not considered as regular coinage.

IRAN

Coins		Current Worth
2 Tomans	Gold	$ 250
1 Toman	Gold	$ 100
Half Toman	Gold	$ 75
Fifth Toman	Gold	$ 25
5 Krans	Silver	$ 40
2 Krans	Silver	$ 10
1 Kran	Silver	$ 5
10 Shahis	Silver	$ 15
5 Shahis	Silver	$ 5
3 Shahis	Silver	$ 3
2 Shahis	Nickel	$ 1.25
1 Shahi	Nickel	65¢

IRAN (*cont.*)

		Current Worth
Coins		

New Coinage

Coins	Metal	Current Worth
10 Pahlevi	Gold	$1,750
5 Pahlevi	Gold	$ 600
2 1/2 Pahlevi	Gold	$ 400
2 Pahlevi	Gold	$ 275
1 Pahlevi	Gold	$ 175
10 Rials	Silver	$ 12.50
5 Rials	Silver	$ 6.50
2 Rials	Silver	$ 2.75
1 Rial	Silver	$ 2
50 Dinars	Aluminum	65¢
10 Dinars	Aluminum	15¢
5 Dinars	Aluminum	10¢
2 Dinars	Bronze	$ 1.50
1 Dinar	Bronze	$ 1.50

Other Coinage

Coins	Metal	Current Worth
20 Rials	Copper-Nickel	$ 1
10 Rials	Copper-Nickel	75¢
5 Rials	Copper-Nickel	50¢
2 Rials	Copper-Nickel	35¢
1 Rial	Copper-Nickel	25¢

The Islamic Republic of Iran is the western and larger half of the great Iranian Plateau between the rivers Indus and Tigris in southwestern Asia. It is bounded on the north by the Union of Soviet Socialist Republics and the Caspian Sea, on the east by Afghanistan and Pakistan, on the south by the Arabian Sea and the Persian Gulf, on the west by Iraq and Turkey.

One Dirhem Showing Altar of Fire Worshippers
(Silver), 600–800 A.D., worth—Rare

50 Dinars (Copper), 1888, worth $10

5 Krans (Silver), 1880 worth $120

IRAQ

Coins		Current Worth
5 Dinars (5000 Fils)	Gold	$300
1 Dinar (1000 Fils)	Silver	$ 32.50
500 Fils	Silver	$ 35
500 Fils	Nickel	$ 7.50
250 Fils	Nickel	$ 4
100 Fils	Copper-Nickel	$ 1.50
50 Fils	Copper-Nickel	75¢
25 Fils	Copper-Nickel	40¢
10 Fils	Copper-Nickel	35¢
5 Fils	Copper-Nickel	20¢

Later Coinage

Riyal (200 Fils)	Silver	$ 25
100 Fils	Silver	$ 10
Dirhem (50 Fils)	Silver	$ 5
25 Fils	Silver	$ 2.50
20 Fils	Silver	$ 2
10 Fils	Copper-Nickel	30¢
5 Fils	Copper-Nickel	25¢
4 Fils	Nickel or Bronze	$ 1
2 Fils	Bronze	60¢
1 Fil	Bronze	20¢

IRELAND

Coins		Current Worth
10 Shillings	Silver	$ 17.50
Half Crown	Silver	$ 5
1 Florin	Silver	$ 12.50
1 Shilling	Silver	$ 10

IRELAND (*cont.*)

Coins		Current Worth
6 Pence	Nickel	$ 1.75
3 Pence	Nickel	$ 1.25
1 Penny	Bronze	$ 1
Halfpenny	Bronze	$ 1
1 Farthing	Bronze	$ 1

Later Coinage

Half Crown	Copper-Nickel	$ 1.50
1 Florin	Copper-Nickel	$ 1
1 Shilling	Copper-Nickel	50¢
3 Pence	Copper-Nickel	25¢
2 Pence	Bronze	20¢
1 Penny	Bronze	15¢
1 Farthing	Bronze	15¢

Decimal Values

50 New Pence	Copper-Nickel	$ 1.75
10 New Pence	Copper-Nickel	35¢
5 New Pence	Copper-Nickel	20¢
2 New Pence	Bronze	15¢
1 New Penny	Bronze	10¢
Half New Penny	Bronze	10¢

Ireland is an island in the Atlantic Ocean near the European mainland. Eire is a sovereign independent republic separated from Great Britain on the east by the Irish Sea and the North Channel, and on the southeast by St. George's Channel.

Thirty Shillings (Brass), 1906, worth—Rare
"Gun Money" issued in base metal

ISLE OF MAN

Coins		Current Worth
50 New Pence	Copper-Nickel	$ 1.50
1 Crown (25 New Pence)	Copper-Nickel	$ 1.25
10 New Pence	Copper-Nickel	35¢
5 New Pence	Copper-Nickel	25¢
2 New Pence	Bronze	20¢
1 New Penny	Bronze	15¢
Half Penny (New)	Bronze	50¢

A self-governing Dependency of the United Kingdom, the Isle of Man is situated in the Irish Sea. Except for a few minor coins issued more than a century ago, it used British currency until 1970, when its own coinage was established on the new decimal system. British and Irish coins also circulate freely on the island.

ISRAEL
(Formerly Palestine, a British Mandate)

Coins		Current Worth
500 Prutahs	Silver	$ 25
250 Pruthas	Silver	$ 12.50
250 Prutahs	Copper-Nickel	$ 2.50
100 Pruthas	Copper-Nickel	$ 1.25
50 Prutahs	Copper-Nickel	65¢
25 Prutahs	Copper-Nickel	40¢
10 Prutahs	Bronze	75¢
5 Pruthas	Bronze	50¢
1 Prutah	Aluminum	50¢
25 Mils	Aluminum	$ 15

New Coinage System

1 Pound	Copper-Nickel	$ 1.50
Half Pound	Copper-Nickel	$ 1
25 Agoroth	Copper-Nickel	50¢
10 Agoroth	Copper-Nickel	20¢
5 Agoroth	Copper-Nickel	10¢
1 Agora	Aluminum	10¢

Variation in Design

25 Agoroth	Aluminum Alloy	50¢
10 Agoroth	Aluminum Alloy	30¢
5 Agoroth	Aluminum Alloy	20¢
1 Agora	Aluminum Alloy	10¢

The Republic of Israel, created in 1948, occupies the major portion of Palestine. It lies on the western edge of Asia bordering on the Mediterranean Sea. It is bounded on the north by Lebanon and Syria, on the east by Jordan, and on the south by Sinai, Egypt.

Many types of commemorative coins have been issued by Israel from 1968 on. These include half-shekel and 1 pound coins in copper-nickel; 5 pound and 10 pound coins in silver; and gold commemoratives with values of 20, 50, 100, and 200 pounds. All of these command premium prices and are highly prized by collectors.

Israeli Commemorative Issues

Coins		Current Worth
500 Pounds	Gold	$600
200 Pounds	Gold	$550
200 Pounds	Silver	$ 50
100 Pounds	Gold	$400
100 Pounds	Silver	$ 35
50 Pounds	Gold	$250
50 Pounds	Silver	$ 25
25 Pounds	Silver	$ 17.50
25 Pounds	Copper-Nickel	$ 7.50
10 Pounds	Silver	$ 12.50
10 Pounds	Copper-Nickel	$ 5
5 Pounds	Silver	$ 10
5 Pounds	Nickel	$ 5
1 Pound	Copper-Nickel	$ 3.50

Commemorative coins consist of many varieties, some bringing higher prices according to the number minted. All are in extremely fine condition or better.

ITALY

Coins		Current Worth
100 Lire	Gold	$450
50 Lire	Gold	$250
20 Lire	Gold	$150

ITALY (*cont.*)

Coins		Current Worth
10 Lire	Gold	$ 85
5 Lire	Gold	$ 85
5 Lire	Silver	$ 17.50
2 Lire	Silver	$ 8.50
1 Lira	Silver	$ 5
50 Centesimi	Silver	$ 3
50 Centesimi	Nickel	75¢
20 Centesimi	Nickel	60¢
10 Centesimi	Copper	$ 1.25
5 Centesimi	Copper	60¢
2 Centesimi	Copper	60¢
1 Centesimo	Copper	85¢
*20 Lire	Silver	$ 60
*10 Lire	Silver	$ 15
5 Lire (Small size)	Silver	$ 5

Coinage of Republic
After World War II

1000 Lire	Silver	$ 17.50
500 Lire	Silver	$ 12.50
200 Lire	Bronze	$ 1.50
100 Lire	Steel	75¢
50 Lire	Steel	50¢
20 Lire	Aluminum	25¢
10 Lire	Aluminum	20¢
5 Lire	Aluminum	15¢
2 Lire	Aluminum	10¢
1 Lira	Aluminum	10¢

Note: Introduction of 20 and 10 silver lire marked a devaluation of the currency during the period between World Wars I and II.

Coins of 2 lire, 1 lira and lesser denominations appeared in various metals including steel, but ran close to those listed, in terms of current worth. Coins of the Italian Republic (dates from 1946 on) represent a further revaluation and also vary in sizes.

The Republic of Italy occupies the entire Italian peninsula stretching from the Alps southeast into the Mediterranean Sea, including the islands of Sicily, Sardinia, Elba and about seventy smaller ones. On the east is the Adriatic Sea, on the south the Mediterranean, on the west between the mainland and Sicily and Sardinia is the Tyrrhenian Sea, and farther north the Ligurian Sea. The Maritime Alps on the west separate it from France, the Swiss Alps on the north from Switzerland, and the Dolomite Alps separate it from Austria, while the Carnac and Julian Alps on the east separate it from Yugoslavia.

John the Baptist Coins of Florence, 12th Century,
stamped in gold, silver, and bronze, worth—Very Rare

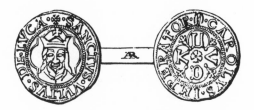

Charles IV Coin of Lucca (Silver),
about 1396, worth—Rare

Sequin of Venice (Gold,) about 1700, worth $800

Double Once of Naples (Gold), 1769, worth $400

Once of Sicily (Gold), 1736, worth $450

Doppia of Sardinia (Gold), 1711, worth $1000

Half Doppia of Sardinia (Gold), 1790, worth $2500

Ducat (Gold), 1784, worth $250

One Soldo (Copper), 1808, worth $1
Kingdom of Napoleon

Ten Centesimi (Copper), 1862, worth $1.50

Twenty Centesimi (Nickel), 1908, worth $1.50

Ducat of Pius VII (Gold), 1800-1823, worth $250

Ducat of Clement XIII (Gold), 1766, worth $250

Sede Vacante Ducat (Gold), 1740, worth $20

Ducat of Pius VI (Gold), 1783, worth $150

Four Soldi (Copper), 1868, worth $4

JAMAICA

Coins		Current Worth
5 Shillings	Copper-Nickel	$ 2.50
Pence	Nickel and Brass	25¢
Halfpence	Nickel and Brass	25¢
Farthings	Nickel and Brass	25¢

Decimal Values

100 Dollars	Gold	$175
25 Dollars	Silver	$125
20 Dollars	Gold	$175
10 Dollars	Silver	$ 45
10 Dollars	Copper-Nickel	$ 12.50
5 Dollars	Silver	$ 45
5 Dollars	Copper-Nickel	$ 6.50
1 Dollar	Copper-Nickel	$ 3.50
50 Cents	Copper-Nickel	$ 1
25 Cents	Copper-Nickel	50¢
20 Cents	Copper-Nickel	40¢
10 Cents	Copper-Nickel	20¢
5 Cents	Copper-Nickel	15¢
1 Cent	Bronze	10¢

Jamaica is situated in the Caribbean Sea ninety miles south of Cuba and is the largest of the British West Indies.

One Penny (Nickel), 1871, worth $5

JAPAN

Coins		Current Worth
1000 Yen	Silver	$ 35
500 Yen	Copper-Nickel	$ 3.50
100 Yen	Copper-Nickel	50¢
50 Yen (hole in center)	Copper-Nickel	25¢
20 Yen	Gold	$800
10 Yen	Gold	$375
5 Yen	Gold	$300
1 Yen	Silver	$ 30
50 Sen	Silver	$ 10
20 Sen	Silver	$ 7.50
10 Sen	Silver	$ 3
5 Sen	Nickel	50¢
1 Sen	Copper	50¢
5 Rin	Copper	25¢
100 Yen	Silver	$ 2
50 Yen	Nickel	$ 1.25
50 Yen	Copper-Nickel	35¢
10 Yen	Bronze	25¢
5 Yen	Brass	15¢
1 Yen	Brass	15¢

Japan consists of four islands which lie in the North Pacific Ocean off the coast of China.

Tempo Money (Copper), before 1867, worth $2.50

One Yen (Silver), 1874-1880, worth $4.25

Two Sen (Copper), 1873-1884, worth $2

JERSEY
(See Guernsey)

Coins		Current Worth
5 Shillings	Copper-Nickel	$ 2
Quarter Shilling	Nickel-Brass	25¢
Twelfth Shilling	Bronze	35¢
Twenty-Fourth Shilling	Bronze	50¢
Forty-Eighth Shilling	Bronze	$ 17.50

Decimal System

50 Pounds	Gold	$500
25 Pounds	Gold	$250
10 Pounds	Gold	$125
5 Pounds	Gold	$ 65
2 1/2 Pounds	Silver	$ 30
2 Pounds	Silver	$ 25
1 Pound	Silver	$ 12.50
50 Pence	Silver	$ 6
50 Pence	Copper-Nickel	$ 1.25
25 Pence	Copper-Nickel	$ 1
10 Pence	Copper-Nickel	35¢
5 Pence	Copper-Nickel	15¢
2 Pence	Bronze	10¢
1 Penny	Bronze	10¢
1/2 Penny	Bronze	10¢

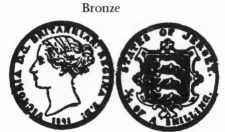

1/26 of Shilling (Copper), 1841, worth $10

JORDAN

Coins		Current Worth
Half Dinar (500 Fils)	Copper-Nickel	$ 6.75
Quarter Dinar (250 Fils)	Copper-Nickel	$ 3.50
100 Fils	Copper-Nickel	$ 2
50 Fils	Copper-Nickel	$ 1
25 Fils	Copper-Nickel	75¢
20 Fils	Copper-Nickel	60¢
10 Fils	Bronze	50¢
5 Fils	Bronze	25¢
1 Fil	Bronze	15¢

Jordan is a constitutional monarchy in Asia Minor, bounded on the north by Syria, on the east by Iraq, on the south by Saudi Arabia, and on the west by Israel.

KENYA

Coins		Current Worth
5 Shillings	Brass	$ 5
2 Shillings	Copper-Nickel	$ 1
1 Shilling	Copper-Nickel	50¢
50 Cents	Copper-Nickel	35¢
25 Cents	Copper-Nickel	25¢
10 Cents	Nickel-Brass	15¢
5 Cents	Nickel-Brass	10¢

The Republic of Kenya is a former British Colony and Protectorate, located on the east coast of Africa, with the equator crossing its very center. It is bounded by Somalia, Sudan, Uganda and Tanzania, with a shore line on Lake Victoria.

KOREA

Coins		Current Worth
Half Won (50 Chon)	Silver	$ 35
20 Chon	Silver	$ 17.50
10 Chon	Silver	$ 10
5 Chon	Nickel	$ 2.50
1 Chon	Copper	$ 1.50
Half Chon	Copper	$ 1

The Republic of Korea occupies a mountainous peninsula in northeastern Asia dividing the Yellow Sea from the Sea of Japan.

Five Yang (Silver), 1894, worth $5

KOREA, NORTH

Coins		Current Worth
10 Chon	Aluminum	$ 1
5 Chon	Aluminum	75¢
1 Chon	Aluminum	50¢

KOREA, SOUTH

Coins		Current Worth
100 Hwan	Nickel	$ 1.25
50 Hwan	Nickel	75¢
10 Hwan	Copper	50¢

Later Coinage

500 Won	Copper-Nickel	$ 7.50
100 Won	Copper-Nickel	$ 1.50
50 Won	Copper-Nickel	75¢
10 Won	Brass or Bronze	35¢
5 Won	Brass or Bronze	20¢
1 Won	Brass	20¢
1 Won	Aluminum	15¢

Silver and gold coins have been issued in proof form in denominations from 50 to 25,000 won but are not regarded as regular coinage.

KUWAIT

Coins		Current Worth
5 Dinar	Gold	$300
2 Dinar	Silver	$ 20
100 Fils	Copper-Nickel	$ 1
50 Fils	Copper-Nickel	50¢
20 Fils	Copper-Nickel	35¢
10 Fils	Nickel-Brass	25¢
5 Fils	Nickel-Brass	15¢
1 Fil	Nickel-Brass	10¢

Kuwait is an Arab state at the head of the Persian Gulf, bordering on Iraq and Saudi Arabia. Formerly a British Protectorate, it is now ruled by a local sheik.

LAOS

Coins		Current Worth
50 Centimes	Aluminum	35¢
20 Centimes	Aluminum	15¢
10 Centimes	Aluminum	10¢

Formerly a part of French Indo-China, Laos later became an independent monarchy. It is a landlocked country, bounded on the north by Burma and China, on the east by Vietnam, on the south by Cambodia, and on the west by Thailand.

LATVIA

Coins		Current Worth
5 Lati	Silver	$ 27.50
2 Lati	Silver	$ 12.50
1 Lati	Silver	$ 7.50
50 Santimi	Nickel	$ 1.50
20 Santimi	Nickel	$ 1
10 Santimi	Nickel	75¢
5 Santimi	Bronze	75¢
2 Santimi	Bronze	75¢
1 Santim	Bronze	50¢

Latvia, a former Russian province, became an independent republic in 1918, but in 1918 was incorporated by the USSR as the Latvian Soviet Socialist Republic. It borders on the Baltic Sea.

LEBANON

Coins		Current Worth
50 Piastres	Silver	$ 10
25 Piastres	Aluminum-Bronze	75¢
25 Piastres	Silver	$ 6
10 Piastres	Silver	$ 4.50
10 Piastres	Aluminum	$ 1.50
5 Piastres	Aluminum	$ 1.25
2 1/2 Piastres	Aluminum	$ 1
1 Piastre	Zinc	75¢
Half Piastre	Zinc	50¢

Later Coinage

1 Livre	Nickel	$ 1.50
50 Piastres	Nickel	75¢
25 Piastres	Nickel-Brass	40¢
10 Piastres	Nickel-Brass	25¢
10 Piastres	Copper-Nickel	35¢
5 Piastres	Nickel-Brass	15¢

Lebanon is a republic in Asia Minor, occupying a strip along the Mediterranean coast, bounded by Syria on the north and east and by Israel on the south.

LIBERIA

Coins		Current Worth
50 Cents	Silver	$ 1.50
25 Cents	Silver	$ 1
10 Cents	Silver	50¢
5 Cents	Copper-Nickel	25¢
2 Cents	Copper-Nickel	$ 1

LIBERIA (*cont.*)

Coins		Current Worth
1 Cent	Copper-Nickel	$ 1
Half Cent	Copper-Nickel	50¢
Half Cent	Brass	30¢

Later Coinage

25 Dollars	Gold	$475
20 Dollars	Gold	$375
10 Dollars	Gold	$300
5 Dollars	Gold	$150
2 1/2 Dollars	Gold	$ 75
5 Dollars	Silver	$ 30
1 Dollar	Silver	$ 20
1 Dollar	Copper-Nickel	$ 2
50 Cents	Copper-Nickel	$ 1.25
25 Cents	Copper-Nickel	65¢
10 Cents	Copper-Nickel	35¢
5 Cents	Copper-Nickel	20¢
1 Cent	Bronze	10¢

The independent Negro Republic of Liberia lies on the south-west Guinea coast of Africa between Sierra Leone (British) on the west and the French colony of the Ivory Coast on the east, with a coast line on the South Atlantic Ocean.

One Cent (Copper), 1847, worth $15

One Cent (Copper), 1833, worth $18

LIBYA

Coins		Current Worth
2 Piastres	Copper-Nickel	75¢
1 Piastre	Copper-Nickel	50¢
5 Milliemes	Bronze	25¢
2 Milliemes	Bronze	20¢
1 Millieme	Bronze	10¢

Later Coinage

100 Milliemes	Copper-Nickel	$ 1
50 Milliemes	Copper-Nickel	50¢
20 Milliemes	Copper-Nickel	40¢
10 Milliemes	Copper-Nickel	20¢
5 Milliemes	Copper-Nickel	15¢
1 Millieme	Nickel-Brass	10¢

Libya, formerly under Italian rule, is a constitutional monarchy on the northern coast of Africa. It is bounded on the north by the Mediterranean Sea, on the east by Egypt, on the south by Sudan and on the west by Tunisia and Algeria.

LIECHTENSTEIN

Coins		Current Worth
100 Franken	Gold	$1,750
50 Franken	Gold	$ 250
25 Franken	Gold	$ 200
20 Franken	Gold	$ 200
10 Franken	Gold	$ 120
5 Franken	Silver	$ 350
2 Franken	Silver	$ 60
1 Franken	Silver	$ 45
Half Franken	Silver	$ 35
20 Kronen	Gold	$2,500
10 Kronen	Gold	$2,500
5 Kronen	Silver	$ 85
2 Kronen	Silver	$ 15
1 Kronen	Silver	$ 10

Liechtenstein is a tiny principality of only 62 square miles, situated on the Upper Rhine between Austria and Switzerland.

LITHUANIA

Coins		Current Worth
10 Litai	Silver	$ 25
5 Litai	Silver	$ 12.50
2 Litai	Silver	$ 6
1 Litai	Silver	$ 2
50 Centu	Aluminum Bronze	$ 1.50
20 Centu	Aluminum Bronze	$ 1.25
10 Centu	Aluminum Bronze	$ 1
5 Centu	Bronze or Aluminum Bronze	$ 1.50

LITHUANIA (*cont.*)

Coins		Current Worth
2 Centu	Bronze or Aluminum Bronze	$ 2
1 Centu	Bronze or Aluminum Bronze	$ 1

Lithuania, an independent Baltic state since the thirteenth century, was forcibly incorporated into the Union of Soviet Socialist Republics in 1940.

LUXEMBOURG

Coins		Current Worth
250 Francs	Silver	$125
100 Francs	Silver	$ 25
50 Francs	Silver	$ 12.50
20 Francs	Silver	$ 7.50
10 Francs	Silver	$ 12.50
5 Francs	Silver	$ 6.50
1 Franc	Nickel	60¢
50 Centimes	Nickel	35¢
25 Centimes	Different Metals	25¢
10 Centimes	Different Metals	25¢
5 Centimes	Different Metals	25¢

Later Coinage

10 Francs	Nickel	40¢
5 Francs	Copper-Nickel	20¢
1 Franc	Copper-Nickel	20¢
20 Centimes	Aluminum	10¢

Luxembourg is a Grand Duchy of Europe, bounded by Germany on the east, Belgium on the north and west, and France on the south.

MACAO

Coins		Current Worth
5 Patacas	Silver	$ 12.50
1 Pataca	Silver	$ 2.50
50 Avos	Nickel	50¢
10 Avos	Bronze	50¢
5 Avos	Bronze	50¢

Later Coinage

1 Pataca	Nickel	$ 1
10 Avos	Nickel-Brass	15¢
5 Avos	Nickel-Brass	10¢

Macao is a Portuguese dependency of only 6 square miles in area, located on an island at the mouth of the Canton River in China.

MALAGASY REPUBLIC
(Madagascar)

Coins		Current Worth
20 Francs	Aluminum	$ 2
10 Francs	Aluminum	$ 1.25
5 Francs	Aluminum	$ 1
2 Francs	Aluminum	75¢

MALAGASY REPUBLIC (*cont.*)

Coins		Current Worth
1 Franc	Aluminum	50¢
1 Franc	Bronze	$ 3
50 Centimes	Bronze	$ 1.50

Later Coinage

20 Francs	Aluminum-Bronze	$ 1.25
10 Francs	Aluminum-Bronze	75¢
5 Francs	Chrome Steel	50¢
2 Francs	Chrome Steel	30¢
1 Franc	Chrome Steel	15¢

The Malagasy Republic occupies the island of Madagascar, off the southeast coast of Africa. It was formerly a French protectorate.

MALAWI

Coins		Current Worth
1 Crown	Copper-Nickel-Zinc	$ 5
Half Crown	Copper-Nickel-Zinc	$ 1.50
1 Florin	Copper-Nickel-Zinc	$ 1
1 Shilling	Copper-Nickel-Zinc	50¢
6 Pence	Copper-Nickel-Zinc	25¢
1 Penny	Bronze	10¢

MALAWI (*cont.*)

Coins		Current Worth
New Decimal Values		
250 Kwacha	Gold	$650
10 Kwacha	Silver	$ 35
5 Kwacha	Silver	$ 27.50
1 Kwacha	Copper-Nickel	$ 1.50
20 Tambala	Copper-Nickel	35¢
10 Tambala	Copper-Nickel	20¢
5 Tambala	Copper-Nickel	15¢
2 Tambala	Bronze	10¢
1 Tambala	Bronze	10¢

Malawi, a republic within the British Commonwealth, was formerly the British Protectorate of Nyasaland. Its coinage supplanted that used by the Federation of Rhodesia and Nyasaland, which is listed under that heading. It follows the western shore of Lake Nyasa, also known as Lake Malawi. It is separated from Rhodesia by Zambia, formerly Northern Rhodesia. Federation coinage is still currently used.

MALAYA
(Including British Borneo)

Coins		Current Worth
50 Cents	Copper-Nickel	$ 1
20 Cents	Copper-Nickel	50¢
10 Cents	Copper-Nickel	30¢
5 Cents	Copper-Nickel	25¢
1 Cent	Bronze	15¢

Malaya occupies a peninsula in Southeast Asia, including the former Straits Settlements. It lies between the Bay of Bengal and the South China Sea and is bounded on the north by Thailand and Burma.

MALAYSIA

Coins		Current Worth
250 Dollars	Gold	$200
200 Dollars	Gold	$175
100 Dollars	Gold	$100
25 Dollars	Silver	$ 35
15 Dollars	Silver	$ 25
10 Dollars	Silver	$ 12.50
5 Dollars	Copper-Nickel	$ 2.75
1 Dollar	Copper-Nickel	$ 1.50
50 Sen	Copper-Nickel	50¢
20 Sen	Copper-Nickel	25¢
10 Sen	Copper-Nickel	20¢
5 Sen	Copper-Nickel	15¢
1 Sen	Copper-Nickel	10¢

Malaysia is a federation of eleven states occupying the southern part of the Malay peninsula in southeast Asia, plus the former British North Borneo (also known as Sabah) and the former British Colony of Sarawak. These are on the island of Borneo, to the east.

MALDIVE ISLANDS

Coins		Current Worth
100 Rufiyaa	Silver	$ 40
25 Rufiyaa	Silver	$ 17.50
20 Rufiyaa	Silver	$ 15
15 Rufiyaa	Silver	$ 12.50
5 Rufiyaa	Copper-Nickel	$ 4.50
50 Lari	Nickel-Brass	$ 1.25
25 Lari	Nickel-Brass	75¢
10 Lari	Nickel-Brass	50¢
5 Lari	Nickel-Brass	35¢
2 Lari	Bronze	25¢
1 Lari	Bronze	20¢

The Maldive Islands are a new republic located in the Indian Ocean southwest of the island of Ceylon. They were formerly a British dependency.

MALI

Coins		Current Worth
100 Francs	Aluminum	$ 2.50
50 Francs	Aluminum	$ 1.50
25 Francs	Aluminum	$ 1.25
10 Francs	Aluminum	50¢
5 Francs	Aluminum	25¢

The Republic of Mali is an island nation situated in the western part of Africa. It was formerly a French possession.

MALTA

Coins		Current Worth
100 Pounds	Gold	$600
50 Pounds	Gold	$300
25 Pounds	Gold	$150
20 Pounds	Gold	$120
10 Pounds	Gold	$ 60
5 Pounds	Silver	$ 60
4 Pounds	Silver	$ 20
2 Pounds	Silver	$ 10
50 Cents	Copper-Nickel	$ 3
10 Cents	Copper-Nickel	$ 1.25
5 Cents	Copper-Nickel	75¢
2 Cents	Copper-Nickel	50¢
1 Cent	Bronze	25¢
5 Mils	Aluminum	20¢
3 Mils	Aluminum	15¢
1 Mil	Aluminum	10¢

Malta, an island 58 miles due south of Sicily in the Mediterranean Sea, and about 180 miles from Africa, was annexed to the British Empire in 1814 following the Napoleonic Wars, and it has been made into a base for repair and refitment of the British fleet and air force.

MAURITANIA

Coins		Current Worth
500 Ouguiya	Gold	$500
20 Ouguiya	Copper-Nickel	$ 12
10 Ouguiya	Copper-Nickel	$ 10
5 Ouguiya	Aluminum-Bronze	$ 7.50
1 Ouguiya	Aluminum-Bronze	$ 6.50
1 Khoum	Aluminum	$ 10

The Republic of Mauritania is a former French possession on the West African Coast, bounded by Spanish Sahara, Algeria, Mali, and Senegal.

MAURITIUS

Coins		Current Worth
1000 Rupees	Gold	$700
200 Rupees	Gold	$350
50 Rupees	Silver	$ 25
25 Rupees	Silver	$ 12.50
10 Rupees	Silver (Proof only)	$350
1 Rupee	Silver	$ 12.50
Half Rupee	Silver	$ 5
Quarter Rupee	Silver	$ 6.50
20 Cents	Silver	$ 5
10 Cents	Silver	$ 5

MAURITIUS (*cont.*)

Coins		Current Worth
	Later Coinage	
1 Rupee	Copper-Nickel	$ 1.50
Half Rupee	Copper-Nickel	$ 1
Quarter Rupee	Copper-Nickel	75¢
10 Cents	Copper-Nickel	25¢
5 Cents	Bronze	20¢
2 Cents	Bronze	15¢
1 Cent	Bronze	10¢

Mauritius, formerly a British possession, is an island in the Indian Ocean, 500 miles east of Madagascar. The island of Mauritius is now an independent nation within the British Commonwealth.

Fifty Sous (Base Silver, 1882, worth $50)

MEXICO

Coins		Current Worth
50 Pesos	Gold	$800
20 Pesos	Gold	$350
10 Pesos	Gold	$175
5 Pesos	Gold	$ 87.50
2 1/2 Pesos	Gold	$ 45
2 Pesos	Gold	$ 35

MEXICO (*cont.*)

Coins		Current Worth
1 Peso	Silver	$ 12.50
50 Centavos	Silver	$ 7.50
20 Centavos	Silver	$ 3
10 Centavos	Silver	$ 2
5 Centavos	Nickel	$ 1
5 Centavos	Bronze	75¢
2 Centavos	Bronze	50¢
1 Centavo	Bronze	20¢

Later Coinage

| | |
---|---|---
100 Pesos | Silver | $ 20
25 Pesos | Silver | $ 15
10 Pesos | Silver | $ 25
5 Pesos | Silver | $ 12.50
1 Peso | Copper-Nickel | 35¢
50 Centavos | Copper-Nickel | 20¢
25 Centavos | Copper-Nickel | 15¢
20 Centavos | Copper-Nickel | 15¢
10 Centavos | Copper-Nickel | 10¢
5 Centavos | Brass | 10¢
1 Centavo | Brass | 10¢

The Republic of Mexico is bounded on the north and northeast by the United States; on the east by the Gulf of Mexico, Gulf of Campeche and the Caribbean Sea; on the south by Guatemala and British Honduras; and on the southwest and west by the Pacific Ocean.

The memory of Hidalgo has been glorified on the gold coinage of Mexico since 1905, on the pieces for 2 1/2, 5 and 10 pesos. Numismatically the father of the country fared better than Dona Josefa Ortiz de Dominguez, through whose efforts the liberation movement was saved from being quelled. She was the wife of the Spanish-Colonial Governor of Queretaro, and both she and her husband were in sympathy with the movement for independence. On December 28, 1942, a five-centavo bronze coin bearing the portrait of Dona Josefa was authorized by presidential decree. This coinage is outstanding because (1) it is the second issue of republican Mexico in which the effigy of a patriot appears, (2) it is the first time a woman was so honored, and (3) the striking of these pieces actually began on December 19, 1942, ten days before its authorization.

Eight Reales (Silver), 1778, worth—Very Rare

One Peso (Silver), 1860, worth $50

One Peso (Silver), 1899, worth $25

One Peso (Silver), 1922, worth $12

MONACO

50 Francs, 1950

MONACO (*cont.*)

Coins		Current Worth
200 Francs	Gold	$650
100 Francs	Gold	$650
100 Francs	Copper-Nickel	$ 5
50 Francs	Silver	$ 37.50
50 Francs	Aluminum-Bronze	$ 4.50
20 Francs	Gold	$150
20 Francs	Aluminum-Bronze	$ 2
10 Francs	Silver	$ 25
10 Francs	Aluminum-Bronze	$ 2.50
5 Francs	Silver	$ 12
5 Francs	Aluminum	$ 1.50
1 Franc	Aluminum	$ 1
1 Franc	Nickel	$ 1
Half Franc	Nickel	75¢
50 Centimes	Aluminum	50¢
20 Centimes	Aluminum-Bronze	20¢
10 Centimes	Aluminum-Bronze	15¢

Monaco is a small principality on the Mediterranean Sea surrounded on all but the ocean side by the French Department of the Maritime Alps.

Five Centimes (Copper), 1838, worth $7.50

MONGOLIA

Coins		Current Worth
750 Tukhrik	Gold	$600
50 Tukhrik	Silver	$ 45
25 Tukhrik	Silver	$ 25
10 Tukhrik	Copper-Nickel	$ 22.50
1 Tukhrik	Copper-Nickel	$ 17.50
1 Tukhrik	Aluminum-Bronze	$ 10
50 Mongo	Silver	$ 12.50
50 Mongo	Copper-Nickel	$ 2.50
20 Mongo	Silver	$ 4.50
20 Mongo	Copper-Nickel	$ 2.50
20 Mongo	Aluminum	$ 2
15 Mongo	Silver	$ 4
15 Mongo	Copper-Nickel	$ 1.75
15 Mongo	Aluminum	$ 1.75
10 Mongo	Silver	$ 3.50
10 Mongo	Copper-Nickel	$ 1.50
10 Mongo	Aluminum	$ 1.50
5 Mongo	Aluminum	$ 1.50
5 Mongo	Copper	$ 7.50
2 Mongo	Aluminum	$ 1
2 Mongo	Copper	$ 5
1 Mongo	Aluminum	75¢
1 Mongo	Copper	$ 5

An ancient country that became a Chinese province in the late 1600s, Mongolia declared its independence in 1911 and later established the Mongolian People's Republic in 1921. It is located between China and Russia.

MOROCCO

Coins		Current Worth
1 Rial	Silver	$ 27.50
Half Rial	Silver	$ 13.50
Quarter Rial	Silver	$ 7
Tenth Rial (Dirham)	Silver	$ 2.75
Twentieth Rial	Silver	$ 1.50
10 Mazunas (Fifth Dirham)	Bronze	$ 1
5 Mazunas	Bronze	$ 1
2 Mazunas	Bronze	$ 1.50
1 Mazuna	Bronze	$ 1.75

Decimal Currency

500 Francs	Silver	$ 25
200 Francs	Silver	$ 7.50
100 Francs	Silver	$ 3.75
50 Francs	Aluminum	75¢
20 Francs	Aluminum	50¢
5 Francs	Aluminum	30¢
2 Francs	Aluminum	20¢
1 Franc	Aluminum	15¢
50 Centimes	Aluminum	10¢
50 Centimes	Nickel	35¢
25 Centimes	Copper-Nickel	25¢

Later Coinage

500 Dirhams	Gold	$250
250 Dirhams	Gold	$150
50 Dirhams	Silver	$ 45
5 Dirhams	Copper-Nickel	$ 3.25
1 Dirham	Copper-Nickel	75¢
50 Santimat	Copper-Nickel	50¢
20 Santimat	Brass	30¢

MOROCCO (*cont.*)

Coins		Current Worth
10 Santimat	Brass	20¢
5 Santimat	Brass	15¢
1 Santim	Aluminum	10¢

Morocco, at one time a French and Spanish Protectorate, is bounded on the east by Algeria, on the north by the Mediterranean Sea, on the south by Rio de Oro and Algeria, and on the west by the Atlantic Ocean.

Ten Mazunas (Bronze), 1904, or 1321 by
Mohammedan Calendar, worth $2

Falu (Copper), 1868, or 1285 by Mohammedan Calendar,
worth $2

MOZAMBIQUE

Coins		Current Worth
20 Escudos	Silver	$ 10
20 Escudos	Nickel	$ 3
10 Escudos	Silver	$ 12.50
10 Escudos	Copper-Nickel	$ 1.50
5 Escudos	Silver	$ 6.50
5 Escudos	Copper-Nickel	75¢
2 1/2 Escudos	Silver	$ 3.50
2 1/2 Escudos	Copper-Nickel	50¢
1 Escudo	Nickel-Bronze	$ 1
1 Escudo	Bronze	35¢
50 Centavos	Nickel-Bronze	50¢
50 Centavos	Bronze	75¢
20 Centavos	Bronze	35¢
20 Centavos	Bronze (smaller)	15¢
10 Centavos	Bronze	30¢
10 Centavos	Bronze (smaller)	10¢

The People's Republic of Mozambique was formerly a Portuguese overseas province on the southeast coast of Africa. It is bounded on the north by Tanganyika and on the west by Rhodesia and the Union of South Africa.

MUSCAT AND OMAN
(See Oman)

Coins		Current Worth
100 Baizah	Copper-Nickel	$ 1
50 Baizah	Copper-Nickel	60¢
25 Baizah	Copper-Nickel	30¢
10 Baizah	Bronze	15¢
5 Baizah	Bronze	10¢
2 Baizah	Bronze	10¢

The independent monarchy of Muscat and Oman follows the southeast coastline of the Arabian peninsula along the Arabian Sea and the Gulf of Oman, with a point of land at the entrance to the Persian Gulf.

NEPAL

Coins		Current Worth
1000 Rupees	Gold	$750
50 Rupees	Silver	$ 35
25 Rupees	Silver	$ 20
20 Rupees	Silver	$ 7.50
10 Rupees	Silver	$ 7.50
1 Rupee	Silver	$ 4.50
1 Rupee	Copper-Nickel	$ 1
50 Paisa	Silver	$ 2.50
50 Paisa	Copper-Nickel	50¢
25 Paisa	Silver	$ 1.25
25 Paisa	Copper-Nickel	35¢
20 Paisa	Brass	35¢
10 Paisa	Various Metals	25¢
5 Paisa	Aluminum	25¢
2 Paisa	Aluminum	20¢
1 Paisa	Aluminum	15¢

All the above are of recent mintage. Earlier coins include Rupees 2, 1, 1/2, 1/4, and 1/6, in gold, which bring premium prices, as do many silver coins of lesser values. Obsolete coins are found in many odd values.

Nepal is an independent monarchy situated amid the Himalaya Mountains along the northeast border of India, with Tibet (now controlled by China) forming its outer boundary.

NETHERLANDS

Coins		Current Worth
10 Gulden (Florins)	Gold	$150
5 Gulden (Florins)	Gold	$450
2 1/2 Gulden	Silver	$ 15
1 Gulden	Silver	$ 7.50
Half Gulden	Silver	$ 5
25 Cents	Silver	$ 4
10 Cents	Silver	$ 1.50
5 Cents	Nickel	65¢
2 1/2 Cents	Bronze	$ 2.50
1 Cent	Bronze	10¢
Half Cent	Bronze	10¢
10 Gulden	Silver	$ 15
2 1/2 Gulden	Nickel	$ 1.25
1 Gulden	Nickel	50¢
25 Cents	Nickel	40¢
10 Cents	Nickel	25¢
5 Cents	Bronze	10¢
1 Cent	Bronze	10¢

The Netherlands, a kingdom in northwestern Europe, is bounded by Germany on the east, Belgium on the south, and the North Sea on the west and north.

Double Ducat or 14 Gulden (Gold), 1750, worth $600

Ducat (Gold), 1801, worth $150

2 1/2 Cents (Copper), 1884, worth $7.50

NETHERLANDS ANTILLES

Coins		Current Worth
200 Gulden	Gold	$175
100 Gulden	Gold	$135
50 Gulden	Gold	$ 75

NETHERLANDS ANTILLES (*cont.*)

Coins		Current Worth
25 Gulden	Silver	$ 40
10 Gulden	Silver	$ 17.50
2 1/2 Gulden	Silver	$ 17.50
2 1/2 Gulden	Nickel	$ 4.50
1 Gulden	Silver	$ 7.50
1 Gulden	Nickel	$ 2
Quarter Gulden	Silver	$ 2.50
25 Cents (1/4 G)	Nickel	75¢
Tenth Gulden	Silver	$ 1.50
10 Cents (1/10 G)	Nickel	35¢
5 Cents	Copper-Nickel	25¢
2 1/2 Cents	Bronze	25¢
1 Cent	Bronze	15¢

The Netherlands Antilles include the islands of Curacao, Bonaire and Aruba, off the coast of South America, along with three islands farther north. Local government is on equality with that of the Netherlands.

NEW CALEDONIA

Coins		Current Worth
100 Francs	Nickel-Bronze	$ 3
50 Francs	Nickel	$ 1.50
20 Francs	Nickel	75¢
10 Francs	Nickel	50¢
5 Francs	Aluminum	$ 1
2 Francs	Aluminum	50¢
1 Franc	Aluminum	25¢
50 Centimes	Aluminum	15¢

New Caledonia is a French Overseas Territory consisting of a group of islands 1000 miles east of Australia and 1000 miles northwest of New Zealand, in the Pacific Ocean.

NEWFOUNDLAND

Coins		Current Worth
2 Dollars	Gold	$125
50 Cents	Silver	$ 15
25 Cents	Silver	$ 7.50
20 Cents	Silver	$ 5
10 Cents	Silver	$ 3
5 Cents	Silver	$ 2.50
1 Cent	Bronze (large)	$ 1.25
1 Cent	Bronze (small)	50¢

This North American British colony voted to confederate with the Dominion of Canada on July 22, 1948.

One Cent (Copper), 1865, worth $2.50

NEW GUINEA

Coins		Current Worth
1 Shilling	Silver	$ 5
6 Pence	Copper-Nickel	$ 5
3 Pence	Copper Nickel	$ 3
1 Penny	Copper-Nickel	$400
Half Penny	Copper-Nickel	$400

New Guinea, which occupies the northeast quarter of an island of the same name, includes other island groups and is part of the Republic Papua New Guinea.

NEW HEBRIDES

Coins		Current Worth
100 Francs	Silver	$ 20
50 Francs	Nickel	$ 1.50
20 Francs	Nickel	$ 1
10 Francs	Nickel	50¢
5 Francs	Nickel-Brass	25¢
2 Francs	Nickel-Brass	15¢
1 Franc	Nickel-Brass	15¢

The New Hebrides are a group of islands 250 miles northeast of New Caledonia in the Pacific Ocean. They are administered jointly by France and England.

NEW ZEALAND

Coins		Current Worth
1 Crown	Silver	$ 25
Half Crown	Silver	$ 10
1 Florin	Silver	$ 10
1 Shilling	Silver	$ 5
6 Pence	Silver	$ 3
3 Pence	Silver	$ 1.75
1 Crown	Copper-Nickel	$ 13.50
Half Crown	Copper-Nickel	$ 1.25
1 Florin	Copper-Nickel	$ 1
1 Shilling	Copper-Nickel	75¢
6 Pence	Copper-Nickel	50¢
3 Pence	Copper-Nickel	25¢
1 Penny	Bronze	30¢
Half Penny	Bronze	25¢

New Decimal Values

1 Dollar	Copper-Nickel	$ 2.50
50 Cents	Copper-Nickel	$ 1.25
20 Cents	Copper-Nickel	50¢
10 Cents	Copper-Nickel	35¢
5 Cents	Copper-Nickel	25¢
2 Cents	Bronze	15¢
1 Cent	Bronze	10¢

New Zealand comprises a group of islands, 1200 miles east of Australia in the South Pacific. It is a self-governing member of the British Commonwealth of Nations.

NEW ZEALAND (*cont.*)

NICARAGUA

Coins		Current Worth
2000 Cordobas	Gold	$350
1000 Cordobas	Gold	$175
500 Cordobas	Gold	$100
200 Cordobas	Gold	$ 45
100 Cordobas	Silver	$ 25
50 Cordobas	Silver	$ 12.50
20 Cordobas	Silver	$ 6.50
1 Cordoba	Silver	$ 35
50 Centavos	Silver	$ 15
25 Centavos	Silver	$ 6
20 Centavos	Silver	$ 4.50
10 Centavos	Silver	$ 2.75
5 Centavos	Silver	$ 5
1 Centavo	Bronze	20¢
Half Centavo	Bronze	15¢

Later Coinage

1 Cordoba	Copper-Nickel	$ 1.25
50 Centavos	Copper-Nickel	50¢
25 Centavos	Copper-Nickel	25¢

NICARAGUA (*cont.*)

Coins		Current Worth
10 Centavos	Various Metals	15¢
5 Centavos	Various Metals	10¢
2 Centavos	Brass	75¢

The Republic of Nicaragua, the largest state in Central America, lies between the Caribbean Sea and the Pacific Ocean, bounded by Honduras on the north and Costa Rica on the south.

One Cordoba (Silver), 1912, worth $35

Five Centavos (Nickel), 1912, worth $2

NIGERIA

Coins		Current Worth
2 Shillings	Copper-Nickel	$ 1.50
1 Shilling	Copper-Nickel	75¢
6 Pence	Copper-Nickel	35¢
3 Pence	Nickel-Brass	20¢
2 Penny	Nickel-Brass	10¢
Half Penny	Nickel-Brass	10¢

New Decimal Values

Coins		Current Worth
25 Kobo	Copper-Nickel	$ 1.75
10 Kobo	Copper-Nickel	$ 1
5 Kobo	Copper-Nickel	50¢
1 Kobo	Bronze	25¢
Half Kobo	Bronze	15¢

Nigeria is a federated republic within the British Commonwealth. It was formerly part of British West Africa and is situated northeast of the Gulf of Guinea.

NORWAY

Coins		Current Worth
20 Kroner	Gold	$450
10 Kroner	Gold	$400
2 Kroner	Silver	$ 50

NORWAY (*cont.*)

Coins		Current Worth
1 Krone	Silver	$ 25
50 Ore	Silver	$ 12.50
25 Ore	Silver	$ 10
10 Ore	Silver	$ 5
5 Ore	Bronze	30¢
2 Ore	Bronze	25¢
1 Ore	Bronze	25¢

Later Coinage

200 Kroner	Silver	$ 50
50 Kroner	Silver	$ 25
25 Kroner	Silver	$ 25
10 Kroner	Silver	$ 20
5 Kroner	Copper-Nickel	$ 2.50
1 Krone	Copper-Nickel	75¢
50 Ore	Copper-Nickel	50¢
25 Ore	Copper-Nickel	25¢
10 Ore	Copper-Nickel	15¢
5 Ore	Bronze	10¢
2 Ore	Bronze	10¢
1 Ore	Bronze	10¢

Norway occupies the west part of the Scandinavian Peninsula in northwest Europe, from the Skagerrak, which separates it from Denmark, to the North Cape in the Arctic Ocean, where on the east it meets Finland and the Union of Soviet Socialist Republics.

Five Ore (Copper), 1876, worth $5

OMAN
(Formerly Muscat and Oman)

Coins		Current Worth
75 Rials	Gold	$650
5 Rials	Silver	$ 40
2 1/2 Rials	Silver	$ 25
1 Rial	Silver	$ 10
Half Rial	Copper-Nickel	$ 1.25
50 Baizah	Copper-Nickel	65¢
25 Baizah	Copper-Nickel	40¢
10 Baizah	Bronze	25¢
5 Baizah	Bronze	15¢

The Sultanate of Oman is located at the southeast tip of the Arabian peninsula originally known as Muscat and Oman. Its name was changed in 1970 and a new currency introduced that same year, with 1000 baizah equalling 1 rial.

PAKISTAN

Coins		Current Worth
1 Rupee	Nickel	$ 1.50
Half Rupee	Nickel	$ 1
Quarter Rupee	Nickel	50¢
2 Annas	Copper-Nickel	35¢
1 Anna	Copper-Nickel	25¢
Half Anna	Copper-Nickel	15¢
1 Pice	Bronze	10¢

New Decimal Values

1 Rupee	Copper-Nickel	$ 1
50 Paisa	Nickel	50¢
25 Paisa	Nickel or Copper-Nickel	25¢

PAKISTAN (*cont.*)

Coins		Current Worth
10 Paisa	Copper-Nickel	15¢
5 Paisa	Nickel-Brass	15¢
2 Paisa	Bronze or Aluminum	10¢
1 Paisa	Various Metals	10¢

Gold and Silver Currency

3000 Rupees	Gold	$650
1000 Rupees	Gold	$200
500 Rupees	Gold	$100
100 Rupees	Silver	$ 30

The Dominion of Pakistan, one of the largest countries in the world, comprises two zones in the northeast and northwest corners of the Indo-Pakistan subcontinent, separated by a thousand miles of territory of the Republic of India. Pakistan was formed by the partition of the subcontinent of India on August 15, 1947, on the basis of the Islamic faith of the majority of the population.

PANAMA

Coins		Current Worth
1 Balboa	Silver	$ 25
Half Balboa	Silver	$ 10
50 Centesimos	Silver	$ 30
25 Centesimos	Silver	$ 25
10 Centesimos	Silver	$ 17.50
5 Centesimos	Silver	$ 7.50
2 1/2 Centesimos	Silver	$ 15
2 1/2 Centesimos	Copper-Nickel	$ 3
Half Centesimo	Copper-Nickel	$ 2.50

PANAMA (*cont.*)

Coins		Current Worth
Later Coinage		
500 Balboas	Gold	$800
150 Balboas	Platinum	$400
100 Balboas	Gold	$160
75 Balboas	Gold	$135
20 Balboas	Silver	$120
10 Balboas	Silver	$ 45
5 Balboas	Silver	$ 25
5 Balboas	Copper-Nickel-clad	$ 5
Half Balboa	Clad-Silver	$ 2.50
Quarter Balboa	Silver	$ 5
Quarter Balboa	Copper-Nickel-clad	50¢
Tenth Balboa	Silver	$ 2.50
Tenth Balboa	Copper-Nickel-clad	25¢
5 Centesimos	Copper-Nickel	10¢
1 Centesimo	Bronze	10¢
2 1/2 Centesimos	Nickel	$ 3
Half Centesimo	Nickel	$ 2.50

The Republic of Panama occupies the entire isthmus connecting Central and South America, lying between the Caribbean Sea on the north and the Pacific Ocean on the south, by Colombia on the east and Costa Rica on the west.

One Half Balboa (Silver), 1904, worth $30

2 1/2 Centesimos (Nickel), 1907, worth $3

PAPAL STATES
(See Italy)

PAPUA - NEW GUINEA

Coins		Current Worth
100 Kina	Gold	$250
10 Kina	Silver	$ 50
10 Kina	Copper-Nickel	$ 40
5 Kina	Silver	$ 25
5 Kina	Copper-Nickel	$ 13.50
1 Kina	Copper-Nickel	$ 7.50
20 Toea	Copper-Nickel	60¢
10 Toea	Copper-Nickel	30¢
5 Toea	Copper-Nickel	20¢
2 Toea	Bronze	15¢
1 Toea	Bronze	10¢

Formerly administered by Australia, Papua is an independent state located on the island of New Guinea and a member of the British Commonwealth.

PARAGUAY

Coins		Current Worth
1 Peso	Silver	$100
Coinage After 1900		
10 Pesos	Copper-Nickel	$ 6.50
5 Pesos	Copper-Nickel	$ 5
2 Pesos	Copper-Nickel	$ 1.75
2 Pesos	Aluminum	$ 1.75
1 Peso	Copper-Nickel	$ 1
50 Centavos	Copper-Nickel	75¢
50 Centavos	Aluminum	75¢
20 Centavos	Copper-Nickel	$ 1.25
10 Centavos	Copper-Nickel	$ 1
5 Centavos	Copper-Nickel	75¢
New Coinage (1944 on)		
50 Guaranies	Steel	$ 1.25
10 Guaranies	Steel	50¢
5 Guaranies	Steel	25¢
1 Guarani	Steel	15¢
50 Centimes	Aluminum-Bronze	40¢
25 Centimes	Aluminum-Bronze	30¢
15 Centimes	Aluminum-Bronze	25¢
10 Centimes	Aluminum-Bronze	20¢
5 Centimes	Aluminum-Bronze	15¢
1 Centime	Aluminum-Bronze	10¢

Special Coinage

During the early 1970's many types of 150 guaranies were struck in silver, valued at $25 each; also 1500 guaranies gold at $200 each; 3000 guaranies gold at $400 each; 4500 guaranies gold at $600 each and 10,000 guaranies gold at $900 each. These were sold chiefly to collectors.

Paraguay, one of the two inland countries of South America, is bounded on the north by Bolivia and Brazil, on the east by Brazil and Argentina, on the south by Argentina, and on the west by Argentina and Bolivia.

One Peso (Silver), 1889, worth $75

PERU

Coins		Current Worth
1 Libra	Gold	$200
Half Libra	Gold	$100
1 Sol (10 Dineros)	Silver	$ 20
Fifth Sol (2 Dineros)	Silver	$ 4.50
1 Dinero	Silver	$ 2.50
Half Dinero	Silver	$ 1.50
1 Sol	Brass	$ 1
20 Centavos	Brass	50¢

PERU *(cont.)*

Coins		Current Worth
10 Centavos	Brass	20¢
5 Centavos	Brass	15¢
Recent Coinage		
100,000 Soles	Gold	$750
50,000 Soles	Gold	$375
5,000 Soles	Silver	$ 37.50
1,000 Soles	Silver	$ 7.50
400 Soles	Silver	$ 27.50
200 Soles	Silver	$ 22.50
100 Soles	Silver	$ 20
50 Soles	Gold	$450
50 Soles	Silver	$ 18.50
20 Soles	Gold	$185
20 Soles	Silver	$ 12.50
10 Soles	Copper-Nickel	$ 1.50
10 Soles	Brass	85¢
5 Soles	Copper-Nickel	75¢
5 Soles	Brass	50¢
1 Sole	Brass	50¢
25 Centavos	Brass	25¢
20 Centavos	Brass	20¢
10 Centavos	Brass	15¢
5 Centavos	Brass	10¢

Peru, situated on the Pacific coast of South America, is bounded on the north by Ecuador, on the northeast and east by Colombia and Brazil, and on the southeast by Bolivia. At its southernmost tip is the Republic of Chile.

8 Reales (Silver), 1826, now One Sol, worth $25

One Sol (Silver), 1914, worth $25

PHILIPPINE ISLANDS
(Under U.S. Sovereignty)

Coins		Current Worth
1 Peso	Silver	$ 25
50 Centavos	Silver	$ 15
20 Centavos	Silver	$ 12.50
10 Centavos	Silver	$ 3.50
5 Centavos	Copper-Nickel	$ 1

PHILIPPINE ISLANDS (*cont.*)

Coins		Current Worth
1 Centavo	Bronze	75¢
Half Centavo	Bronze	50¢

Under the Republic

1 Peso	Silver	$ 20
50 Centavos	Nickel-Brass	$ 1
25 Centavos	Nickel-Brass	50¢
10 Centavos	Nickel-Brass	25¢

Tagalog Coinage (1967 on)

5,000 Piso	Gold	$1,350
1,500 Piso	Gold	$ 400
1,000 Piso	Gold	$ 225
50 Piso	Silver	$ 25
25 Piso	Silver	$ 15
5 Piso	Nickel	$ 1.25
1 Piso	Gold	$ 375
1 Piso	Silver	$ 25
1 Piso	Nickel	$ 1
1 Piso	Copper-Nickel	35¢
50 Sentimos	Copper-Nickel-Zinc	50¢
25 Sentimos	Copper-Nickel	25¢
10 Sentimos	Copper-Nickel	15¢
5 Sentimos	Brass	10¢
1 Sentimo	Aluminum	10¢

The Republic of the Philippines, largest island group in the Malay Archipelago, consists of 7110 islands extending 1150 statute miles from north to south and 682 miles from east to west in the shape of a huge triangle, 7000 miles from San Francisco.

One Centavo (Copper), 1903, worth $1.50

POLAND

Coins		Current Worth
20 Zloty	Gold	$135
10 Zloty	Gold	$ 70
10 Zloty	Silver	$ 17.50
5 Zloty	Silver	$ 12.50
2 Zloty	Silver	$ 6.50
1 Zloty	Silver	$ 4.50
50 Groszy	Nickel	$ 1.25
20 Groszy	Nickel or Zinc	75¢
10 Groszy	Nickel or Zinc	40¢
5 Groszy	Bronze	30¢
2 Groszy	Bronze	20¢
1 Groszy	Bronze	20¢

Later Coinage

500 Zloty	Gold	$600
200 Zloty	Silver	$ 15
100 Zloty	Silver	$ 12.50
50 Zloty	Silver	$ 10
20 Zloty	Copper-Nickel	$ 2.50
10 Zloty	Copper-Nickel	$ 1
5 Zloty	Aluminum	50¢
1 Zloty	Aluminum	25¢
50 Groszy	Aluminum	15¢
20 Groszy	Aluminum	10¢

POLAND (*cont.*)

Coins		Current Worth
10 Groszy	Aluminum	10¢
5 Groszy	Aluminum	10¢
2 Groszy	Aluminum	10¢
1 Groszy	Aluminum	10¢

Note: Coins of 5 and 10 zloty values appear in various types and designs of a commemorative nature, which bring premium prices.

Poland, a republic in Central Europe, is bounded on the north by the Baltic Sea, East Prussia and Lithuania, both of which are occupied by the Union of Soviet Socialist Republics, on the south by Czechoslovakia, and on the west by East Germany.

Double Ducat (Gold), 1753, worth $800

Ducat (Gold), 1702, worth $750

Ducat (Gold), 1740, worth $650

Five Zloty (Silver), 1831, worth $25

PORTO RICO
(See Puerto Rico)

PORTUGAL

Coins		Current Worth
10,000 Reis	Gold	$375
5,000 Reis	Gold	$200
2,500 Reis	Gold	$125
2,000 Reis	Gold	$ 85
1,000 Reis	Silver	$ 25
500 Reis	Silver	$ 15
200 Reis	Silver	$ 10
100 Reis	Silver	$ 5
100 Reis	Copper-Nickel	$ 1
50 Reis	Silver	$ 3.50

PORTUGAL (*cont.*)

Coins		Current Worth
50 Reis	Copper-Nickel	$ 1
20 Reis	Bronze	$ 2
10 Reis	Bronze	$ 2
5 Reis	Bronze	$ 1

New Monetary System

250 Escudos	Silver	$ 25
100 Escudos	Silver	$ 12.50
50 Escudos	Silver	$ 12.50
25 Escudos	Copper-Nickel	$ 1.25
20 Escudos	Silver	$ 17.50
10 Escudos	Silver	$ 10
5 Escudos	Silver	$ 5
5 Escudos	Copper-Nickel	40¢
2 1/2 Escudos	Silver	$ 2.50
2 1/2 Escudos	Copper-Nickel	25¢
1 Escudo	Silver	$ 27.50
1 Escudo	Aluminum-Bronze	$ 1.25
1 Escudo	Copper-Nickel	50¢
1 Escudo	Bronze	20¢
50 Centavos	Silver	$ 10
50 Centavos	Aluminum-Bronze	$ 1
50 Centavos	Copper-Nickel	$ 1.50
20 Centavos	Bronze	15¢
10 Centavos	Silver	$ 2.50
10 Centavos	Copper-Nickel	30¢
10 Centavos	Bronze or Aluminum	10¢
5 Centavos	Bronze	25¢
4 Centavos	Copper-Nickel	50¢
2 Centavos	Bronze	25¢
2 Centavos	Iron	$ 40
1 Centavo	Bronze	50¢

Portugal occupies the western part of the Iberian Peninsula, bounded on the north and east by Spain and on the south and west by the Atlantic Ocean.

10 Reis (Copper), 1884, worth $2

PORTUGESE GUINEA

Coins		Current Worth
20 Escudos	Silver	$ 8.50
10 Escudos	Silver	$ 4.50
5 Escudos	Copper-Nickel	$ 1
2 1/2 Escudos	Copper-Nickel	60¢
1 Escudo	Nickel-Bronze	$ 2.50
50 Centavos	Nickel-Bronze	$ 1.75
50 Centavos	Bronze	75¢
20 Centavos	Bronze	75¢
10 Centavos	Bronze	$ 2.50
10 Centavos	Aluminum	$ 1
5 Centavos	Bronze	$ 1.50

New Coinage (Republic)

20 Pesos	Copper-Nickel	$ 2.50
5 Pesos	Copper-Nickel	$ 1
2 1/2 Pesos	Copper-Nickel	75¢
1 Peso	Nickel-Brass	50¢
50 Centavos	Aluminum	25¢

Formerly a Portuguese overseas province, Portuguese Guinea declared itself the Republic of Guinea-Bissau in 1979. It is located on the West Coast of Africa, bounded by Senegal on the north and Guinea on the south.

PUERTO RICO

Coins		Current Worth
1 Peso	Silver	$300
40 Centavos	Silver	$150
20 Centavos	Silver	$ 75
10 Centavos	Silver	$ 35
5 Centavos	Silver	$ 20

Puerto Rico is an island in the West Indies, east of Hispaniola. It had its own currency for a brief period until Spain ceded it to the United States in 1898 and since then its coins have greatly increased in value.

One Peso (Silver), 1895, worth $300

QATAR AND DUBAI

Coins		Current Worth
50 Dirhems	Copper-Nickel	75¢
25 Dirhems	Copper-Nickel	40¢
10 Dirhems	Bronze	25¢
5 Dirhems	Bronze	15¢
1 Dirhem	Bronze	10¢

This is one of a group of protected states located on the east of the Arabian peninsula, near the mouth of the Persian Gulf. It is governed by a local sheik.

REUNION ISLAND

Coins		Current Worth
100 Francs	Nickel	$ 2
50 Francs	Nickel	$ 1.50
20 Francs	Aluminum-Bronze	$ 1
10 Francs	Aluminum-Bronze	50¢
5 Francs	Aluminum	35¢
2 Francs	Aluminum	30¢
1 Franc	Aluminum	25¢

Reunion, a French possession, is an island in The Indian Ocean, about 400 miles east of Madagascar.

RHODESIA
(Zimbabwe)

Coins		Current Worth
2 1/2 Shillings (25 Cents)	Copper-Nickel	$ 1.25
2 Shillings (20 Cents)	Copper-Nickel	$ 1
1 Shilling (10 Cents)	Copper-Nickel	50¢
6 Pence (5 Cents)	Copper-Nickel	25¢
3 Pence (2 1/2 Cents)	Copper-Nickel	15¢

Decimal Coinage

2 1/2 Cents	Copper-Nickel	30¢
1 Cent	Bronze	15¢
Half Cent	Bronze	10¢

Originally Southern Rhodesia, in 1953 this territory merged with the neighboring Protectorates of Northern Rhodesia and Nyasaland. In 1963 it became independent under the name of the Republic of Rhodesia, issuing its own coinage. In 1978 it changed its name to the Republic of Zimbabwe. Coinage of the 1953–63 period are still in circulation.

RHODESIA AND NYASALAND

Coins		Current Worth
Half Crown	Copper-Nickel	$ 4.50
1 Florin	Copper-Nickel	$ 2.50
1 Shilling	Copper-Nickel	$ 1.50
6 Pence	Copper-Nickel	$ 1
3 Pence	Copper-Nickel	50¢
1 Penny	Bronze	25¢
Half Penny	Bronze	25¢

The Federation of Rhodesia and Nyasaland lies in the central part of South Africa. It includes Northern Rhodesia and the former protectorate of Nyasaland.

ROMANIA (Rumania)

Coins		Current Worth
100 Lei	Gold	$1,000
50 Lei	Gold	$ 350
25 Lei	Gold	$ 250
20 Lei	Gold	$ 150
5 Lei	Silver	$ 25
2 Lei	Silver	$ 10
1 Leu	Silver	$ 5
50 Bani	Silver	$ 2.50
20 Bani	Copper-Nickel	75¢
10 Bani	Copper-Nickel	50¢
5 Bani	Copper-Nickel	30¢
2 Bani	Copper	75¢
1 Bani	Copper	50¢

Mintage of People's Republic

Coins		Current Worth
20 Lei	Aluminum	$ 15
5 Lei	Aluminum	$ 1
3 Lei	Nickel-clad-Steel	$ 1
2 Lei	Aluminum	$ 1
1 Leu	Aluminum	$ 1
1 Leu	Nickel-clad-Steel	75¢
50 Bani	Copper-Nickel	$ 1.50
25 Bani	Copper-Nickel	75¢
25 Bani	Nickel-clad-Steel	50¢
15 Bani	Nickel-clad-Steel	30¢

ROMANIA (*cont.*)

Coins		Current Worth
10 Bani	Copper-Nickel	50¢
5 Bani	Aluminum-Bronze	50¢
5 Bani	Nickel-clad-Steel	25¢
3 Bani	Aluminum-Bronze	50¢
1 Ban	Aluminum-Bronze	30¢

Romania is bounded on the north by the Union of Soviet Socialist Republics; on the east by the Ukrainian Soviet Socialist Republic, Moldavian Soviet Socialist Republic, and the Black Sea; on the south by Bulgaria; and on the west by Yugoslavia and Hungary.

Ten Bani (Copper), 1867, worth $1.50

250 Lei (Silver), 1937, $12

RUSSIA
(Union of Soviet Socialist Republics)

Coins		Current Worth
10 Roubles	Gold	$175
1 Rouble	Silver	$ 17.50
50 Kopecks	Silver	$ 10
20 Kopecks	Silver	$ 3
15 Kopecks	Silver	$ 2
10 Kopecks	Silver	$ 1.50
5 Kopecks	Copper	$ 3
3 Kopecks	Copper	$ 2.50
2 Kopecks	Copper	$ 2
1 Kopeck	Copper	$ 2
Half Kopeck	Copper	$ 3.50

Revalued Currency

1 Rouble	Copper-Nickel	$ 1.50
50 Kopecks	Copper-Nickel	$ 1
20 Kopecks	Copper-Nickel	75¢
15 Kopecks	Copper-Nickel	50¢
10 Kopecks	Copper-Nickel	35¢
5 Kopecks	Aluminum-Bronze	25¢

RUSSIA (*cont.*)

Coins		Current Worth
3 Kopecks	Brass	20¢
2 Kopecks	Brass	15¢
1 Kopeck	Brass	10¢

The U.S.S.R., in area the largest country in the world, stretches across two continents from the North Pacific Ocean to the Gulf of Finland. It occupies the northern part of Asia and the eastern half of Europe, from the Arctic to the Black Sea. Its western borders brush against Finland, the Baltic Sea, Poland, Czechoslovakia, Hungary, and Rumania. On the south it is bound by Rumania, the Black Sea, Turkey, Iran, Afghanistan, China, Mongolian People's Republic, and Korea. In the far northeast, the Bering Strait separates it from Alaska.

One Rouble (Silver), 1883, worth $45

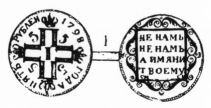

5 Roubles, worth $750

Gold Ducat, worth $500

Gold Ducat, worth $1,200

Five Kopecks (Copper), 1868, worth $2.50

RWANDA

Coins		Current Worth
10 Francs	Copper-Nickel	$ 1.50
5 Francs	Bronze	75¢
1 Franc	Copper-Nickel	50¢
	New Coinage	
200 Francs	Silver	$ 15
50 Francs	Brass	$ 1.75
20 Francs	Brass	$ 1.25
10 Francs	Copper-Nickel	$ 1.25
5 Francs	Bronze	$ 1
2 Francs	Aluminum	75¢
1 Franc	Aluminum	15¢
Half Franc	Aluminum	15¢

The Republic of Rwanda is in east central Africa and has extensive shore lines along both Lake Victoria and Lake Albert.

ST. HELENA

Coins		Current Worth
1 Crown	Silver	$ 35
1 Crown	Copper-Nickel	$ 2
25 Pence	Silver	$ 30
25 Pence	Copper-Nickel	$ 2
1/2 Penny (1821)	Copper	$ 12.50

The island of St. Helena is a British colony more than 1000 miles west of the African coast.

ST. PIERRE AND MIQUELON

Coins		Current Worth
2 Francs	Aluminum	$ 2.50
1 Franc	Aluminum	$ 1.25

St. Pierre and Miquelon are tiny groups of barren islands off the coast of Newfoundland; they are a French possession used as a fishing base.

ST. THOMAS AND PRINCE

Coins		Current Worth
50 Escudos	Silver	$ 10
20 Escudos	Nickel	$ 2.50
10 Escudos	Silver	$ 7.50
10 Escudos	Copper-Nickel	$ 1.50
5 Escudos	Silver	$ 5.50
5 Escudos	Copper-Nickel	$ 1
2 1/2 Escudos	Silver	$ 3.50
2 1/2 Escudos	Copper-Nickel	75¢
1 Escudo	Copper-Nickel	$ 3.50
1 Escudo	Bronze	50¢
50 Centavos	Copper-Nickel	$ 5
50 Centavos	Bronze	35¢
20 Centavos	Nickle-Bronze	$ 2.50
20 Centavos	Bronze	25¢
10 Centavos	Nickel-Bronze	$ 2
10 Centavos	Bronze	15¢
10 Centavos	Aluminum	15¢

St. Thomas and Prince are two islands in the Gulf of Guinea, near the West Coast of Africa. Together, they constituted a Portuguese Overseas Province which became a Republic in 1975.

Old Portuguese coin struck for St. Thomas and Prince

SAN MARINO

Coins		Current Worth
2 Scudo	Gold (1975)	$175
1 Scudo	Gold (1975)	$100
500 Lire	Silver	$ 13.50
100 Lire	Steel	$ 1
50 Lire	Steel	50¢
20 Lire	Gold	$750
20 Lire	Silver	$ 50
20 Lire	Aluminum-Bronze	50¢
10 Lire	Gold	$500
10 Lire	Silver	$ 25
10 Lire	Aluminum	25¢
5 Lire	Silver	$ 5
5 Lire	Aluminum	25¢
2 Lire	Silver	$ 25
2 Lire	Aluminum	25¢
1 Lira	Silver	$ 15
1 Lira	Aluminum	25¢
50 Centesim	Silver	$ 10
10 Centesimi	Copper or Bronze	$ 2.50
5 Centesimi	Copper or Bronze	$ 2.50

San Marino is the world's smallest republic as well as the oldest. It is located in Italy, on the slopes of the Apennine Mountains. Its coinage dates from the 1860s, with a lapse between 1940 and 1970.

SAUDI ARABIA

Coins		Current Worth
1 Guinea (40 Ryals)	Gold	$165
1 Ryal	Silver	$ 15
Half Ryal	Silver	$ 7.50
Quarter Ryal	Silver	$ 3.50
4 Girsh (Fifth Ryal)	Copper-Nickel	50¢
2 Girsh	Copper-Nickel	35¢
1 Girsh	Copper-Nickel	25¢
1 Halala (Fifth Girsh)	Bronze	10¢

Recent Coinage

100 Halala	Copper-Nickel	$ 1.50
50 Halala	Copper-Nickel	$ 1.25
25 Halala	Copper-Nickel	75¢
10 Halala	Copper-Nickel	30¢
5 Halala	Copper-Nickel	15¢

Earlier mintage of 1/4 and 1/2 girsh are valued at $1 to $3 in fine condition.

Saudi Arabia is a kingdom covering most of the Arabian peninsula. Its west coast stretches almost the full length of the Red Sea, while its east coast extends along half of the Persian Gulf. Neighboring states are Jordan and Iraq on the north, Yemen and South Yemen on the south, and Muscat and Oman on the southeast.

SERBIA
(Now part of Yugoslavia)

Coins		Current Worth
20 Dinara	Gold	$135
10 Dinara	Gold	$ 90
5 Dinara	Silver	$ 45
2 Dinara	Silver	$ 10
1 Dinar	Silver	$ 4.50
50 Paras	Silver	$ 2.25
20 Paras	Nickel	$ 2
10 Paras	Nickel	$ 1.50
5 Paras	Nickel	$ 1.50
2 Paras	Bronze	$ 3.50

Two Dinara (Silver), 1875, worth $35

SEYCHELLES

Coins		Current Worth
10 Rupees	Copper-Nickel	$ 5
5 Rupees	Silver	$ 75
5 Rupees	Copper-Nickel	$ 2.50
1 Rupee	Silver	$ 17.50
1 Rupee	Copper-Nickel	$ 1.50
Half Rupee	Silver	$ 17.50
Half Rupee	Copper-Nickel	$ 1
25 Cents	Silver	$ 12.50
25 Cents	Copper-Nickel	$ 1.25
10 Cents	Copper-Nickel	$ 1.50
10 Cents	Nickel-Brass	50¢
5 Cents	Bronze	45¢
2 Cents	Bronze	25¢
1 Cent	Bronze	50¢
5 Cents	Aluminum	25¢
1 Cent	Aluminum	10¢

The Seychelles Islands are a British republic situated in the Indian Ocean 600 miles north of the Island of Madagascar and about 1000 miles east from the African coast.

SIERRA LEONE

Coins		Current Worth
1 Golde	Gold	$1,000
Half Golde	Gold	$ 500
Quarter Golde	Gold	$ 300
2 Leone	Copper-Nickel	$ 14.50
1 Leone	Copper-Nickel	$ 10
50 Cents	Copper-Nickel	$ 1.75
20 Cents	Copper-Nickel	75¢
10 Cents	Copper-Nickel	50¢
5 Cents	Copper-Nickel	25¢
1 Cent	Bronze	15¢
Half Cent	Bronze	10¢

The former British colony of Sierra Leone is a republic situated on the west of Africa with Guinea on the north and Liberia on the south.

SINGAPORE

Coins		Current Worth
500 Dollars	Gold	$650
250 Dollars	Gold	$450
150 Dollars	Gold	$400
100 Dollars	Gold	$150
10 Dollars	Silver	$ 25
5 Dollars	Silver	$ 15
1 Dollar	Copper-Nickel	$ 2
50 Cents	Copper-Nickel	65¢
20 Cents	Copper-Nickel	40¢
10 Cents	Copper-Nickel	20¢
5 Cents	Copper-Nickel	15¢
5 Cents	Aluminum	20¢
1 Cent	Bronze	15¢
1 Cent	Copper-clad-Steel	10¢

Originally the capital city of Straits Settlements, Singapore became a member of the federation of Malaya in 1963, but withdrew two years later to form a republic with its own currency.

The republic of Singapore is situated on an island at the lower tip of the Malay peninsula in Asia.

SOLOMON ISLANDS

Coins		Current Worth
5 Dollars	Silver	$100
5 Dollars	Copper-Nickel	$ 20
1 Dollar	Copper-Nickel	$ 2.50
20 Cents	Copper-Nickel	$ 1
10 Cents	Copper-Nickel	40¢
5 Cents	Copper-Nickel	25¢
2 Cents	Bronze	15¢
1 Cent	Bronze	10¢

A British protectorate since the late nineteenth century, the Solomon Islands in the Southwest Pacific Ocean became self-governing in 1976 and gained full independence in 1978.

SOMALIA

Coins		Current Worth
5 Shillings	Copper-Nickel	$ 2.50
1 Somalo	Silver	$ 2.75
1 Scellino	Copper-Nickel	50¢
50 Centimisi	Silver	$ 2
50 Centimisi	Copper-Nickel	25¢
10 Centimisi	Bronze	25¢
10 Centimisi	Brass	15¢
5 Centimisi	Bronze	10¢
5 Centimisi	Brass	10¢
1 Centimiso	Bronze	10¢

SOMALIA (*cont.*)

Coins		Current Worth
Decimal Coinage		
1 Shilin	Copper-Nickel	60¢
50 Senti	Copper-Nickel	30¢
10 Senti	Aluminum	15¢
5 Senti	Aluminum	10¢

Somalia occupies the extreme eastern point of Africa, extending along the Gulf of Aden and the Indian Ocean. It is composed of the former colonies of British Somaliland and Italian Somaliland.

SOUTH AFRICA
Mintage of the Republic (1961 on)

Coins		Current Worth
1 Krugerrand (Troy ounce)	Gold	$650
2 Rand	Gold	$165
1 Rand	Gold	$ 80
1 Rand	Silver	$ 12.50
1 Rand	Nickel	$ 1.25
50 Cents	Silver	$ 12.50
50 Cents	Nickel	75¢
20 Cents	Silver	$ 5
20 Cents	Nickel	35¢
10 Cents	Silver	$ 2.50
10 Cents	Nickel	20¢
5 Cents	Silver	$ 1.50
5 Cents	Nickel	15¢
2 1/2 Cents	Silver	$ 1.50
2 Cents	Bronze	10¢

SOUTH AFRICA (*cont.*)

Coins		Current Worth
1 Cent	Bronze	10¢
Half Cent	Bronze	10¢
Half Cent	Brass	35¢

Earlier mintage of gold and higher values of silver bring premium prices.

The Republic of South Africa was established in 1961, supplanting the Union of South Africa and its coinage.

SOUTHERN YEMEN

Coins		Current Worth
50 Fils	Copper-Nickel	$ 1
25 Fils	Copper-Nickel	50¢
5 Fils	Bronze	15¢
1 Fil	Bronze	10¢
New Coinage (1971 on)		
5 Fils	Bronze	60¢
5 Fils	Aluminum	30¢
2 1/2 Fils	Aluminum	15¢

Formerly known as South Arabia, this independent nation occupies a strip of land along the southern shore of the Arabian peninsula, including the port of Aden and some islands in the Arabian Sea. Late in 1970, after a change in government, South Yemen became the People's Democratic Republic of Yemen.

SPAIN

Coins		Current Worth
100 Pesetas	Gold	$675
25 Pesetas	Gold	$275
20 Pesetas	Gold	$200
5 Pesetas	Silver	$ 25
2 Pesetas	Silver	$ 20
1 Peseta	Silver	$ 15
50 Centimos	Silver	$ 4.50
10 Centimos	Copper	$ 1
5 Centimos	Copper	50¢

Later Coinage

100 Pesetas	Silver	$ 7.50
50 Pesetas	Copper-Nickel	$ 2
25 Pesetas	Copper-Nickel	$ 1.50
5 Pesetas	Copper-Nickel	50¢
2 1/2 Pesetas	Aluminum	50¢
1 Peseta	Aluminum-Bronze	25¢
50 Centimos	Aluminum	20¢
10 Centimos	Aluminum	15¢
5 Centimos	Aluminum	10¢

Spain is bounded on the west by Portugal and the Atlantic Ocean, on the north by the Atlantic Ocean and France, on the east and south by the Mediterranean Sea. At its southernmost tip is the British fort, Gibraltar.

Five Centimos (Copper), 1867, worth $5.50

SRI LANKA
(Formerly Ceylon)
New Coinage (1973)

Coins		Current Worth
5 Rupees	Nickel	$ 3.50
2 Rupees	Copper-Nickel	$ 1.75
1 Rupee	Copper-Nickel	$ 1.25
50 Cents	Copper-Nickel	60¢
25 Cents	Copper-Nickel	40¢
10 Cents	Nickel-Brass	25¢
5 Cents	Nickel-Brass	20¢
2 Cents	Aluminum	15¢
1 Cent	Aluminum	10¢

STRAITS SETTLEMENTS
(Federated Malay States)
(Now British Malaya, Federation of Malaya)

Coins		Current Worth
Dollar	Silver	$ 35
50 Cents	Silver	$ 10
20 Cents	Silver	$ 5
10 Cents	Silver	$ 2.50
5 Cents	Silver	$ 1.25
5 Cents	Copper-Nickel	$ 2.50
1 Cent	Copper	$ 1
Half Cent	Copper	$ 2
Quarter Cent	Copper	$ 1.25

One Dollar (Silver), 1904, worth $35

After more than a hundred years as a British crown colony, Straits Settlements relinquished that status to join the Malayan Federation. Further coinage will be found under Malaya, Malagasia and Singapore.

SUDAN

Coins		Current Worth
100 Pounds	Gold	$675
50 Pounds	Gold	$350
10 Pounds	Silver	$ 35
5 Pounds	Silver	$ 35
2 1/2 Pounds	Silver	$ 25
50 Piastres (Ghirsh)	Copper-Nickel	$ 5
10 Piastres	Copper-Nickel	$ 1
5 Piastres	Copper-Nickel	60¢
2 Piastres	Copper-Nickel	50¢
10 Milliemes (1 Piastre)	Bronze	25¢
5 Milliemes	Bronze	20¢
2 Milliemes	Bronze	15¢
1 Millieme	Bronze	15¢

Sudan is situated in northeast Africa, directly south of Egypt. It is the largest country in the entire continent and was formerly under British and Egyptian administration, but is now an independent nation.

SURINAM

Coins		Current Worth
100 Gulden	Gold	$145
25 Gulden	Silver	$ 25
10 Gulden	Silver	$ 15
1 Gulden	Silver	$ 10
25 Cents	Copper-Nickel	35¢
10 Cents	Copper-Nickel	15¢
5 Cents	Nickel-Brass	10¢
5 Cents	Aluminum	10¢
1 Cent	Nickel-Brass	10¢
1 Cent	Aluminum	10¢

Surinam, on the north coast of South America, was formerly the colony of Dutch Guiana. Later it had a local government equal to that of the Netherlands and became an independent republic in 1975.

SWAZILAND

Coins		Current Worth
1 Lilangeni	Copper-Nickel	$ 2.50
50 Cents	Copper-Nickel	$ 1.25
20 Cents	Copper-Nickel	60¢
10 Cents	Copper-Nickel	20¢
5 Cents	Copper-Nickel	20¢
2 Cents	Bronze	15¢
1 Cent	Bronze	10¢

Silver and gold coins have been struck in denominations from 10 cents up to 100 Angeni (lilangenis) but are either uncirculated or obtainable in proof form only.

Swaziland is a kingdom in Southeast Africa between the South African Republic and Mozambique.

SWEDEN

Coins		Current Worth
20 Kronor	Gold	$350
10 Kronor	Gold	$150
5 Kronor	Silver	$ 12
1 Krona	Silver	$ 6
50 Ore	Silver	$ 3
25 Ore	Silver	$ 1.50
10 Ore	Silver	$ 1
5 Ore	Copper	30¢
2 Ore	Copper	20¢
1 Ore	Copper	10¢
50 Kronor	Silver	$ 35
10 Kronor	Silver	$ 17.50
5 Kronor	Copper-Nickel	$ 3.50
2 Kronor	Silver	$ 12.50
2 Kronor	Copper-Nickel	75¢
1 Krona	Copper-Nickel	50¢
50 Ore	Copper-Nickel	25¢
25 Ore	Nickel-Bronze	15¢
25 Ore	Copper-Nickel	15¢
10 Ore	Nickel-Bronze	10¢
10 Ore	Copper-Nickel	10¢
5 Ore	Bronze or Iron	10¢
2 Ore	Bronze or Iron	10¢
1 Ore	Bronze or Iron	10¢

Note: Iron was used instead of bronze for 1, 2 and 5 ore coins during World Wars I and II. While most are fairly common, some command prices up to $80.

Sweden occupies the eastern and largest part of the Scandinavian Peninsula in northwest Europe, with Norway on the west and the Gulf of Bothnia and the Tornea River from Finland on the east. The Baltic Sea separates it from the Baltic States and Germany on the southeast and south, and the Kattegat separates it from Denmark on the southwest.

Double Ducat (Gold), 1702, worth $400

Ducat (Gold), 1761, worth $250

Five Ore (Copper), 1889, worth $350

SWITZERLAND

Coins		Current Worth
100 Francs	Gold	$2500
20 Francs	Gold	$ 135
10 Francs	Gold	$ 70
5 Francs	Silver	$ 15
2 Francs	Silver	$ 10
*1 Franc	Silver	$ 5
Half Franc	Silver	$ 3
20 Centimes	Nickel	20¢
10 Centimes	Nickel	15¢
5 Centimes	Nickel	15¢
2 Centimes	Bronze	10¢
1 Centime	Bronze	10¢

Later Coinage (1968 on)

5 Francs	Copper-Nickel	$ 3.50
2 Francs	Copper-Nickel	$ 1.50
1 Franc	Copper-Nickel	75¢
Half Franc	Copper-Nickel	40¢
20 Centimes	Copper-Nickel	15¢
10 Centimes	Copper-Nickel	10¢
5 Centimes	Copper-Nickel	10¢

The Republic of Switzerland in Central Europe is bounded on the west by France, on the north by Germany, on the east by Austria and Italy, and on the south by Italy.

*Reduced in size beginning 1931. Large francs bring prices ranging from $50 in fine condition to $650 for extremely fine.

1 Duplone (Gold), 1796, worth $500

Double Ducat (Zurich) (Gold), 1776, worth $850

16 Livres of Lucerne (Gold), worth $600

Ducat of Zurich (Gold), 1755, worth $500

16 Francs (Gold), 1800, worth $1500

20 Centimes (Nickel), 1885, worth 75¢

2 Centimes (Copper), 1870, worth $25

Bracteates Struck at Berne, 12th Century, worth $2 each

16 Livres (Gold), worth $150

SYRIA

Coins		Current Worth
1 Lira (Pound)	Gold	$150
1 Lira	Silver	$ 7.50
1 Pound	Nickel	$ 1
Half Pound	Gold	$ 75
50 Piastres	Silver	$ 3.50
50 Piastres	Nickel	50¢
25 Piastres	Silver	$ 1.75
25 Piastres	Nickel	35¢
10 Piastres	Silver	$ 1.50
10 Piastres	Copper-Nickel	50¢
10 Piastres	Aluminum-Bronze	25¢
5 Piastres	Copper-Nickel	35¢
5 Piastres	Aluminum-Bronze	20¢
5 Piastres	Brass	15¢
2 1/2 Piastres	Copper-Nickel	25¢
2 1/2 Piastres	Aluminum-Bronze	15¢
2 Piastres	Aluminum-Bronze	$ 4
1 Piastre	Various Metals	$ 1
Half Piastre	Various Metals	$ 1

Coins listed above include those minted during the period 1958-61 while Syria was part of the United Arab Republic and those minted in subsequent years as the separate Syrian Arab Republic.

The Republic of Syria in the Levant is bound on the north by Turkey, on the east by Iraq, on the south by Hashemite Jordan and Israel, and on the west by Lebanon and the Mediterranean Sea.

TAIWAN

Coins		Current Worth
2,000 Dollars	Gold	$750
1,000 Dollars	Gold	$500
100 Dollars	Silver	$ 25
50 Dollars	Silver	$ 15
10 Dollars	Copper-Nickel	$ 1.75
5 Dollars	Copper-Nickel	85¢
1 Dollar	Copper-Nickel	50¢
5 Chiao (50 Cents)	Silver	$ 3.50
5 Chiao	Brass	50¢
2 Chiao	Aluminum	40¢
1 Chiao	Aluminum	20¢
1 Chiao	Bronze	60¢

Taiwan, formerly called Formosa, is a large island off the Chinese mainland between the Philippines in the south and Japan on the north. Taiwan is occupied by the Chinese Nationalist Republic.

TANGANYIKA TERRITORY
(Formerly German East Africa)

Coins		Current Worth
2 German Rupee	Silver	$250
1 German Rupee	Silver	$ 12.50
Half Rupee	Silver	$ 10
Quarter Rupee	Silver	$ 5
10 Heller	Copper-Nickel	$ 15
5 Heller	Copper-Nickel	$ 20
1 Heller	Copper-Nickel	$ 3.50
Half Heller	Copper-Nickel	$ 10
Pesa (1/64)	Copper-Nickel	$ 7.50

Tanganyika, a Trust Territory administered by a governor with executive and legislative councils, formerly was German East Africa. It was taken by the British in 1918, when the Urundi and Ruanda districts were taken by Belgium, and the Kionga Triangle by Mozambique (Portuguese East Africa). Tanganyika extends from the east African coast to Lake Tanganyika and from Lake Nyasa to Victoria Nyanza.

TANZANIA

Coins		Current Worth
5 Shillingi	Copper-Nickel	$ 2.50
1 Shillingi	Copper-Nickel	50¢
50 Senti	Copper-Nickel	35¢
20 Senti	Nickel-Brass	20¢
5 Senti	Bronze	15¢

The Republic of Tanzania consists of the former Republic of Tanganyika and island of Zanzibar, just off the African coast. For previous coinage see Tanganyika and Zanzibar.

THAILAND
(Formerly Siam)

Coins		Current Worth
20 Baht	Silver	$ 20
10 Baht	Silver	$ 7
10 Baht	Nickel	$ 1.75
5 Baht	Copper-Nickel	$ 1.25
2 Baht	Copper-Nickel	$ 1
1 Baht	Copper-Nickel	75¢
50 Satang	Various Metals	50¢
25 Satang	Various Metals	25¢
10 Satang	Various Metals	20¢
5 Satang	Various Metals	20¢
1 Satang	Tin	15¢

Certain dates and various types bring premium prices. Silver and gold coins ranging from 50 baht up to 5000 baht have been specially minted during the decade from 1970 to 1980, mostly of commemorative types.

Thailand, a constitutional monarchy, is situated in southeastern Asia with Burma on its northwest and west, French Indo-China on its northeast and east, and the Gulf of Thailand (part of the China Sea) on its south and east.

The coins of Siam are much sought after. Some of them, known to European travellers as "bullet money," are lumps of gold or silver, hammered by rude implements into a doubtful roundness, with a few Siamese characters stamped irregularly upon them. The sacred elephant is found on a large proportion of their money. One Siamese coin of recent date is quite handsome in both workmanship and design: on the Obverse is the sacred elephant in ponderous proportion, on the Reverse a group of three pagodas.

TIMOR

Coins		Current Worth
10 Escudos	Silver	$ 10
10 Escudos	Copper-Nickel	$ 2
6 Escudos	Silver	$ 7.50
5 Escudos	Copper-Nickel	$ 1.50
3 Escudos	Silver	$ 4
2 1/2 Escudos	Copper-Nickel	75¢
1 Escudo	Copper-Nickel	35¢
60 Centavos	Copper-Nickel	25¢
50 Centavos	Bronze	20¢
30 Centavos	Bronze	15¢
20 Centavos	Bronze	10¢
10 Centavos	Bronze	50¢

Earlier Coinage With Different Values

50 Avos	Silver	$ 7.50
20 Avos	Nickel-Bronze	$ 5
10 Avos	Bronze	$ 2

Timor was a Portuguese colony forming the eastern part of an island of the same name, the rest belonging to Indonesia. In 1975 it became a part of Indonesia, so the currency listed here is now obsolete.

TONGA

Coins		Current Worth
2 Palanga	Copper-Nickel	$ 4
1 Palanga	Copper-Nickel	$ 2
50 Seniti	Copper-Nickel	$ 1
20 Seniti	Copper-Nickel	50¢

TONGA (*cont.*)

Coins		Current Worth
10 Seniti	Copper-Nickel	25¢
5 Seniti	Copper-Nickel	15¢
2 Seniti	Bronze	10¢
1 Seniti	Bronze	10¢

Tonga is a kingdom formed by an extensive island group in the South Pacific, once known as the Society Islands. For many years they were a British Protectorate. The group is south of Samoa and northeast of New Zealand.

TRINIDAD AND TOBAGO

Coins		Current Worth
10 Dollars	Silver	$ 40
5 Dollars	Silver	$ 30
10 Dollars	Copper-Nickel	$ 12
5 Dollars	Copper-Nickel	$ 6
50 Cents	Copper-Nickel	75¢
25 Cents	Copper-Nickel	50¢
10 Cents	Copper-Nickel	20¢
5 Cents	Bronze	15¢
1 Cent	Bronze	10¢

Trinidad and Tobago is an independent nation within the British Commonwealth. It consists of two islands of those names, situated just off the coast of Venezuela, in northeast South America.

TUNISIA

Coins		Current Worth
100 Francs	Copper-Nickel	$ 1
50 Francs	Copper-Nickel	50¢
20 Francs	Copper-Nickel	35¢
5 Francs	Copper-Nickel	25¢
2 Francs	Aluminum-Bronze	50¢
1 Franc	Aluminum-Bronze	35¢
50 Centimes	Aluminum-Bronze	35¢
25 Centimes	Nickel-Bronze	30¢
10 Centimes	Zinc	25¢
5 Centimes	Bronze	25¢

Coinage of the Republic

1 Dinar	Silver	$ 7.50
1 Dinar	Copper-Nickel	$ 5
Half Dinar	Copper-Nickel	$ 2.50
100 Millimes	Brass	50¢
50 Millimes	Brass	35¢
20 Millimes	Brass	25¢
10 Millimes	Brass	20¢
5 Millimes	Aluminum	15¢
2 Millimes	Aluminum	15¢
1 Millime	Aluminum	10¢

Tunisia, a French protectorate since 1881, formerly one of the Barbary States under the suzerainty of Turkey, is situated on the northern coast of Africa with the Mediterranean Sea on the north and east, Libya on the southwest, the Sahara Desert on the south, and Algeria on the west. New values went into effect when Tunisia became a republic in 1957.

8 Caroub (Copper), 1864–1880, worth $10

TURKEY

Coins		Current Worth
1 Lira (100 Piastres)	Gold	$175
Half Lira (50 Piastres)	Gold	$ 7.50
Quarter Lira (25 Piastres)	Gold	$ 45
20 Piastres	Silver	$ 25
10 Piastrea	Silver	$ 15
5 Piastres	Silver	$ 7.50
2 Piastres	Silver	$ 5
1 Piastre (40 Paras)	Silver	$ 4
Half Piastre	Silver	$ 2.50
1 Piastre	Nickel	50¢
20 Paras	Nickel	25¢
10 Paras	Nickel	20¢
5 Paras	Nickel	20¢

New Coinage Following World War II

500 Lira	Gold	$250
200 Lira	Silver	$ 25
100 Lira	Silver	$ 35
50 Lira	Silver	$ 27.50

TURKEY (*cont.*)

Coins		Current Worth
25 Lira	Silver	$ 17.50
10 Lira	Silver	$ 15
5 Lira	Steel	$ 1
2 1/2 Lira	Steel	65¢
1 Lira	Silver	$ 10
1 Lira	Copper-Nickel	$ 1.25
1 Lira	Steel	50¢
50 Kurus	Silver	$ 6.50
50 Kurus	Steel	35¢
25 Kurus	Brass	30¢
25 Kurus	Steel	25¢
10 Kurus	Brass or Bronze	15¢
5 Kurus	Brass or Bronze	10¢
Half Kurus	Brass	$350
25 Kurus	Steel	25¢
10 Kurus	Brass or Bronze	15¢
5 Kurus	Brass or Bronze	15¢
1 Kurus	Brass or Bronze	10¢
Half Kurus	Brass	$350

The Republic of Turkey occupies territory in both Europe and Asia. European Turkey is bounded on the north by the Black Sea, Bulgaria and Greece; on the east by the Black Sea, on the west by the Aegean Sea and Greece. Turkey in Europe is separated from Turkey in Asia by the Bosporus at Istanbul and the Dardanelles. Turkey in Asia is bounded on the east by the Union of Soviet Socialist Republics and Iran; on the south by Iraq, Syria, and the Mediterranean Sea, and on the west by the Mediterranean Sea and the Aegean Sea.

Turkish coins often bear texts from the Koran on either side.

Ten Paras (Copper), 1839-1861, worth $2

TURKS AND CALCOS ISLANDS

Coins		Current Worth
1 Crown	Copper-Nickel	$ 3.50

A British Colony in the West Indies, situated southeast of the Bahamas and north of Haiti.

UGANDA

Coins		Current Worth
5 Shillings	Copper-Nickel	$ 2.50
2 Shillings	Copper-Nickel	$ 1
1 Shilling	Copper-Nickel	50¢
50 Cents	Copper-Nickel	25¢
20 Cents	Bronze	15¢
10 Cents	Bronze	10¢
5 Cents	Bronze	10¢

The Republic of Uganda is a former British Protectorate in east central Africa with extensive shore lines on Lake Victoria to the east, Lake Albert on the west, and with its southern tip touching the north of Lake Tanganyika. Uganda borders on Sudan, Congo, Tanzania and Kenya.

UNION OF SOUTH AFRICA

Coins and paper same as Great Britian. Also the following:

Coins		Current Worth
1 Sovereign	Gold	$175
Half Soverign	Gold	$ 85
5 Shillings	Silver	$ 17.50
2 1/2 Shillings	Silver	$ 12.50
2 Shillings (florin)	Silver	$ 10
1 Shilling	Silver	$ 10
6 Pence	Silver	$ 3
3 Pence	Silver	$ 1.50
1 Penny	Bronze	30¢
Half-Penny	Bronze	20¢
Farthing (quarter penny)	Bronze	15¢

The Union of South Africa, a dominion within the British Commonwealth of Nations, occupies the southern portion of Africa, including the former colonies of the Cape of Good Hope, Natal, the Transvaal, and the Orange Free State.

One Penny (Copper), 1892, worth $10

UNITED ARAB EMIRATES

Coins		Current Worth
1 Dinar	Copper-Nickel	$ 1.50
50 Fils	Copper-Nickel	75¢
25 Fils	Copper-Nickel	50¢
10 Fils	Bronze	25¢
5 Fils	Bronze	20¢
1 Fil	Bronze	10¢

These consist of seven independent oil-producing states located on the Arabian Coast, and using a common currency since 1973.

URUGUAY

Coins		Current Worth
1000 Pesos	Silver	$ 25
10 Pesos	Silver	$ 12.50
1 Peso	Silver	$ 25
50 Centesimos	Silver	$ 12.50
20 Centesimos	Silver	$ 5
10 Centesimos	Silver	$ 3

Other Metals

100 Pesos	Copper-Nickel	$ 1
50 Pesos	Copper-Nickel	75¢
20 Pesos	Copper-Nickel	50¢
10 Pesos	Aluminum-Bronze	35¢
10 Pesos	Nickel-Brass	35¢
5 Pesos	Aluminum-Bronze	35¢
5 Pesos	Nickel-Brass	25¢
1 Peso	Copper-Nickel	75¢
1 Peso	Aluminum-Bronze	25¢
1 Peso	Nickel-Brass	10¢

URUGUAY (*cont.*)

Coins		Current Worth
50 Centesimos	Copper-Nickel	35¢
50 Centesimos	Aluminum	15¢
25 Centesimos	Copper-Nickel	35¢
20 Centesimos	Aluminum	10¢
10 Centesimos	Aluminum-Bronze	75¢
10 Centesimos	Copper-Nickel	25¢
10 Centesimos	Nickel-Brass	10¢

Lesser coins (1, 2, 5 centesimos) of various metals, 10¢ to 25¢.

Coinage Reform
(With dates 1975 and later)
1 New Peso = 1000 Old Pesos

5 New Pesos	Aluminum-Bronze	$ 1.35
1 New Peso	Aluminum-Bronze	60¢
50 Centesimos	Aluminum-Bronze	40¢
20 Centesimos	Aluminum-Bronze	30¢
10 Centesimos	Aluminum-Bronze	20¢
5 Centesimos	Aluminum	15¢

The Republic of Uruguay, the smallest and one of the most advanced republics in South America, is bounded on the north and east by Brazil, on the south by the South Atlantic Ocean and the River Plata, and on the west by Argentina, the boundary line being the River Uruguay.

One Peso (Silver), 1877, worth $25

5 Centesimos (Copper), 1901, worth 25¢

VATICAN CITY

Coins		Current Worth
1000 Lire	Silver	$ 25
500 Lire	Silver	$ 15
200 Lire	Aluminum-Bronze	$ 3.50
100 Lire	Steel	$ 2.50
50 Lire	Steel	$ 2
20 Lire	Aluminum-Bronze	$ 1.25
10 Lire	Aluminum	$ 1
5 Lire	Aluminum	85¢
2 Lire	Aluminum	50¢
1 Lira	Aluminum	40¢

Vatican City is an independent state covering more than 13 acres in Rome. It includes St. Peter's, the Vatican Palace and Museum, and the Vatican Gardens, and neighboring buildings.

VENEZUELA

Coins		Current Worth
100 Bolivares	Gold	$650
50 Bolivares	Silver	$ 37.50
25 Bolivares	Gold	$165
25 Bolivares	Silver	$ 25
20 Bolivares	Gold	$125
10 Bolivares	Gold	$ 62.50
10 Bolivares	Silver	$ 30
5 Bolivares	Silver	$ 25
2 Bolivares	Silver	$ 10
1 Bolivar	Silver	$ 5
50 Centimos	Silver	$ 3
25 Centimos	Silver	$ 1.50
5 Bolivares	Nickel	$ 5
2 Bolivars	Nickel	$ 1
1 Bolivar	Nickel	50¢
50 Centimos	Nickel	25¢
25 Centimos	Nickel	15¢
12 1/2 Centimos	Copper-Nickel	15¢
5 Centimos	Copper-clad-Steel	10¢
5 Centimos	Copper-clad-Nickel	15¢

Venezuela is the northernmost state of South America and is bounded on the north by the Caribbean Sea, on the east by British Guiana, on the southeast by Brazil, and on the west and southwest by Columbia.

Five Bolivars (Silver), 1912, worth $25

VIETNAM
Coinage of North Vietnam

Coins		Current Worth
2 Dong	Bronze	$ 25
1 Dong	Aluminum	$ 25
5 Hao (Half Dong)	Aluminum	$ 10
20 Xu (Fifth Dong)	Aluminum	$ 35
5 Xu	Aluminum	$ 1.50
2 Xu	Aluminum	$ 1.25
1 Xu	Aluminum	$ 1

Coinage of South Vietnam

Coins		Current Worth
20 Dong	Nickel-clad Steel	$ 2
10 Dong	Nickel-clad Steel	75¢
10 Dong	Brass-clad Steel	60¢
5 Dong	Nickel-clad Steel	50¢
5 Dong	Copper-Nickel	65¢

VIETNAM (*cont.*)

Coins		Current Worth
1 Dong	Various Metals	30¢
50 Xu	Aluminum	$ 1.25
50 Su	Aluminum	$ 1.50
20 Su	Aluminum	$ 1
10 Su	Aluminum	50¢
5 Xu	Aluminum	25¢
2 Xu	Aluminum	15¢
1 Xu	Aluminum	10¢

Formerly part of French Indo China, Vietnam declared itself independent following World War II. Rivalry between two factions caused a division of North and South, with each issuing its own currency until 1975 when North Vietnam took full control as the Socialist Republic of Vietnam. The country occupies Southeast Asia on the Chinese Sea.

WESTERN AFRICAN STATES

Coins		Current Worth
500 Francs	Silver	$ 35
100 Francs	Nickel	$ 2
50 Francs	Copper-Nickel	$ 1.25
100 Francs	Nickel	$ 2
25 Francs	Aluminum-Bronze	75¢
10 Francs	Aluminum-Bronze	35¢
5 Francs	Aluminum-Bronze	25¢
1 Franc	Aluminum	15¢

These consist of the independent Republics of Dahomey, Niger, Mauritania, Ivory Coast, Senegal, Sudanese Republic, Togo, and Upper Volta. All are former French colonies in west Africa that use a common currency.

WESTERN SAMOA

Coins		Current Worth
1 Tala	Copper-Nickel	$ 3.50
50 Sene	Copper-Nickel	$ 1.75
20 Sene	Copper-Nickel	75¢
10 Sene	Copper-Nickel	35¢
5 Sene	Copper-Nickel	20¢
2 Sene	Bronze	10¢
1 Sene	Bronze	10¢

Western Samoa is an independent nation formed by four islands of the Samoan group, located more than 2500 miles southwest of Hawaii. A German colony until World War II, the islands were administered by New Zealand until they became fully independent in 1962 and adopted a decimal currency in 1967.

YEMEN
(The Yemen Arab Republic)

Coins		Current Worth
1 Ryal	Silver	$ 8.50
20 Bogach (Half Ryal)	Silver	$ 5
Quarter Ryal	Silver	$ 25
10 Bogach (Quarter Ryal)	Silver	$ 2.50

YEMEN (*cont.*)

Coins		Current Worth
Fifth Ryal (8 Bogach)	Silver	$ 5
5 Bogach (Eighth Ryal)	Silver	$ 1.50
Tenth Ryal	Silver	$ 2.50
Twentieth Ryal	Silver	$ 2
2 Bogach (Twentieth Ryal)	Brass-Bronze	$ 1
1 Bogach	Brass or Bronze	$ 1
1 Bogach	Aluminum-Bronze	35¢
Half Bogach	Bronze	$ 3.50
Half Bogach	Aluminum-Bronze	25¢
1 Halala (Half Bogach)	Bronze	35¢

These supplanted earlier coins (prior to 1962) of similar values, which are worth two to three times as much as current coins (except for the 1/4 ryal). Older values had the name ahmadi or imadi, as the equivalent of the ryal. They included two five-sided coins, the 1/8 ahmadi (worth $2.) and the 1/16 ahmadi (worth $1.) and a six-sided 1/8 ahmadi, worth $50 or more.

Decimal Coinage

1 Ryal	Copper-Nickel	$ 5
50 Fils	Copper-Nickel	75¢
25 Fils	Copper-Nickel	50¢
10 Fils	Brass	25¢
5 Fils	Brass	15¢

Yemen is an independent Republic in southwest Arabia, fronting on the Red Sea. Formerly governed by Turkey, it was established as a monarchy following World War I, until it became a republic in 1967.

YUGOSLAVIA
From World War I to World War II

Coins		Current Worth
4 Dukata	Gold	$350
1 Dukat	Gold	$ 85
50 Dinara	Silver	$ 18.50
50 Dinara	Aluminum-Bronze	$ 3.50
20 Dinara	Gold	$125
20 Dinara	Silver	$ 7.50
20 Dinara	Aluminum-Bronze	$ 1.25
10 Dinara	Silver	$ 3.75
10 Dinara	Nickel	$ 1.75
2 Dinara	Nickel-Bronze	$ 1
2 Dinara	Aluminum-Bronze	75¢
1 Dinar	Nickel-Bronze	75¢
1 Dinar	Aluminum-Bronze	50¢
50 Para	Nickel-Bronze	50¢
50 Para	Aluminum-Bronze	50¢
25 Para	Nickel-Bronze	$ 1.25
10 Para	Zinc	$ 3
5 Para	Zinc	$ 15

Federated Republic (1945 on)

50 Dinara	Aluminum-Bronze	75¢
20 Dinara	Aluminum-Bronze	35¢
10 Dinara	Aluminum-Bronze	30¢
10 Dinara	Copper-Nickel	65¢
5 Dinara	Aluminum	30¢
5 Dinara	Copper-Nickel	35¢
2 Dinara	Aluminum	20¢
2 Dinara	Copper-Nickel	30¢
1 Dinara	Aluminum	20¢
1 Dinara	Copper-Nickel	30¢
50 Para	Aluminum	15¢

YUGOSLAVIA (*cont.*)

Coins		Current Worth
50 Para	Copper-Zinc	20¢
20 Para	Copper-Zinc	25¢
10 Para	Copper-Zinc	15¢
5 Para	Copper-Zinc	10¢

The Balkan kingdom of Yugoslavia, formed by Serbia, Pontenegro, and various Slavic territories in 1918, became a Federated Republic in 1945, with Serbia, Croatia, Slovenia, the Bosnia-Herzegovina, Macedonia, and Montenegro as its autonomous components. It occupies the Adriatic coast of Europe's Balkan peninsula.

ZAIRE

Coins		Current Worth
5 Makuta	Copper-Nickel	$ 2
1 Likuta	Copper-Nickel	$ 1.25
10 Sengi	Aluminum	75¢
10 Francs	Aluminum	$ 1

The Democratic Republic of Congo is in the heart of equatorial Africa. It is surrounded by half a dozen other countries and some of the continent's largest lakes lie along its eastern border. It was formerly the Belgian Congo. In 1971 the name of the country was officially changed to the Republic of Zaire.

ZAMBIA

Coins		Current Worth
5 Shillings	Copper-Nickel	$ 3.50
2 Shillings	Copper-Nickel	$ 1.50
1 Shilling	Copper-Nickel	75¢
6 Pence	Copper-Nickel	35¢
1 Penny	Bronze	10¢

ZAMBIA (*cont.*)
Coins

Current
Worth

New Decimal Coinage (1968 on)

50 Ngwee	Copper-Nickel	$ 2.50
20 Ngwee	Copper-Nickel	$ 1
10 Ngwee	Copper-Nickel	50¢
5 Ngwee	Copper-Nickel	25¢
2 Ngwee	Bronze	10¢
1 Ngwee	Bronze	10¢

The Republic of Zambia was formed from the British Protectorate of Northern Rhodesia; but first, it became part of the Central African Federation, which included Rhodesia and Nyasaland, with coinage minted under that title from 1953 to 1963. (See page 240.) The Zambian Republic was established in 1964, and has had its own coinage since that date, but the currency of Rhodesia and Nyasaland remained in circulation. However, the decimal coinage introduced in 1968 has rendered previous issues obsolete. Zambia is separated from Rhodesia by the Zambezi River, famous for the great Victoria Falls.

ZANZIBAR

Coins

Current
Worth

Rial	Silver	$200
Pessa	Copper	$ 1.50

Decimal Coinage

20 Cents	Nickel	$300
10 Cents	Bronze	$250
5 Cents	Bronze	$200

Zanzibar, an island of 640 square miles off the eastern coast of Africa, became an independent nation and was admitted to the United Nations on December 16, 1963. The neighboring island of Pemba is included as part of Zanzibar, which had been a British Protectorate since 1890. In 1964, Zanzibar and Pemba joined with Tanganyika to form the Republic of Tanzania. The decimal coinage became obsolete and rose rapidly in value.

ZIMBABWE

Coins		Current Worth
5 Pounds	Gold	$700
1 Pound	Gold	$250
10 Shillings	Gold	$125
2 1/2 Shillings (25 Cents)	Copper-Nickel	$ 1.25
2 Shillings (20 Cents)	Copper-Nickel	$ 1
1 Shilling (10 Cents)	Copper-Nickel	50¢
6 Pence (5 Cents)	Copper-Nickel	25¢
3 Pence (2 1/2 Cents)	Copper-Nickel	15¢

Decimal Coinage

25 Cents	Copper-Nickel	$ 1.25
20 Cents	Copper-Nickel	$ 1
10 Cents	Copper-Nickel	60¢
2 1/2 Cents	Copper-Nickel	30¢
1 Cent	Bronze	15¢
Half Cent	Bronze	10¢

Originally Southern Rhodesia, in 1953 this territory merged with the neighboring Protectorates of Northern Rhodesia and Nyasaland.

In 1963, it became independent as the Republic of Rhodesia, again issuing its own coinage and in 1978 its name was changed to Zimbabwe - Rhodesia.

APPENDIX

NEWEST LISTINGS
AND
NEW COUNTRIES
IN ALPHABETICAL ORDER

AFGHANISTAN
Coinage of Republic (1973–1978)

Coins		Current Worth
500 Afghani	Silver	$ 45
250 Afghani	Silver	$ 25
5 Afghani	Clad Steel	75¢
50 Puli	Clad Steel	35¢
75 Puli	Clad Steel	20¢

Coinage of Democratic Republic (1978 on)

500 Afghani	Silver	$ 35
5 Afghani	Brass	$ 3.50
5 Afghani	Copper-Nickel	$ 2.50
50 Puli	Aluminum	75¢
25 Puli	Aluminum	60¢

ANDORRA

Coins		Current Worth
1 Diner	Silver	$ 30
1 Diner (100 Pesetas)	Brass	$ 2.50

Andorra is a small semi-independent state in the Pyrenees Mountains between Spain and France.

ANGOLA

(People's Republic 1875 on)

Coins		Current Worth
20 Kwanzas	Copper-Nickel	$ 5
10 Kwanzas	Copper-Nickel	$ 3
5 Kwanzas	Copper-Nickel	$ 1.50
2 Kwanzas	Copper-Nickel	75¢
1 Kwanza	Copper-Nickel	50¢
50 Lwei	Copper-Nickel	30¢

ASCENSION ISLAND

Coins		Current Worth
1 Crown	Silver	$ 25
1 Crown	Copper-Nickel	$ 5

Ascension Island is a British base in the Atlantic Ocean northwest of St. Helena.

BAHAMAS

Coins		Current Worth
2,500 Dollars*	Gold	$5,750
250 Dollars	Gold	$ 750

*Twice the width of a U.S. half dollar.

BELIZE

Coins		Current Worth
250 Dollars	Gold Commemorative	$250
100 Dollars	Gold (ten different coins, each with a different historical symbol)	$100 to $350
50 Dollars	Gold	$ 85
25 Dollars	Silver	$ 35

BENIN

(See Dahomey)

CHINA

(People's Republic 1980s)

Coins		Current Worth
1 Yuan (10 Jiao)	Copper-Nickel	$ 1.25
5 Jiao	Copper-Nickel	65¢
2 Jiao	Copper-Nickel	25¢
1 Jiao (10 cents)	Copper-Nickel	15¢
5 Cents*	Aluminum	15¢
2 Cents*	Aluminum	10¢
1 Cent*	Aluminum	10¢

*Earlier dates run higher (See Page 105)

CHILE

Latest Coinage

Coins		Current Worth
1 Onza	Gold	$ 500
500 Pesos	Gold	$1,500
100 Pesos	Gold	$ 250
50 Pesos	Gold	$ 275
50 Pesos	Aluminum	$ 2.50
10 Pesos	Silver	$ 100

DAHOMEY

Coins		Current Worth
25,000 Francs	Gold	$2,500
10,000 Francs	Gold	$1,000
5,000 Francs	Gold	$ 500
2,500 Francs	Gold	$ 250
1,000 Francs	Silver	$ 100
500 Francs	Silver	$ 50
200 Francs	Silver	$ 22.50
100 Francs	Silver	$ 12.50

A former French colony located between Togo and Nigeria in Africa, Dahomey became independent in 1960 and coined its own gold and silver in 1971. In 1972 a new regime took power and in 1975 the name of the republic was changed to BENIN.

FAEROE ISLANDS

(See Denmark for Regular Coinage)

The following coins, dated 1941, were specially minted in England during World War II and have become collector's items, in fine condition or better:

Coins		Current Worth
25 Ore	Copper-Nickel	$ 10
10 Ore	Copper-Nickel	$ 8
5 Ore	Bronze	$ 6
2 Ore	Bronze	$ 6
1 Ore	Bronze	$ 10

These islands are located in the North Atlantic Ocean, halfway between Scotland and Iceland. They have been a Danish possession for 600 years, but were under British protection during World War II and were granted home rule in 1948.

FALKLAND ISLANDS

Coins		Current Worth
50 Pence	Copper-Nickel	$ 2.50
20 Pence	Copper-Nickel	50¢
10 Pence	Bronze	40¢
5 Pence	Bronze	30¢
2 Pence	Bronze	15¢
1 Penny	Bronze	10¢
Half Penny	Bronze	10¢

Special 1983 Coinage
(150th year of British Rule)

FALKLAND ISLANDS (*cont.*)

Coins		Current Worth
50 Pence	Gold	$1,600
50 Pence	Silver	$ 50
50 Pence	Copper	$ 6

All coins with receded edge: *proofs only.*

A British colony in the South Atlantic Ocean 300 miles east of the Straits of Magellan.

GUINEA-BISSAU

(See Portuguese Guinea)

GOA

(Portuguese India)

Final Decimal Coinage
(1958–1961)

Coins		Current Worth
6 Escudos	Copper-Nickel	$ 5.50
3 Escudos	Copper-Nickel	$ 3.75
1 Escudo	Copper-Nickel	$ 2
60 Centavos	Copper-Nickel	$ 1.25
30 Centavos	Bronze	75¢
10 Centavos	Bronze	35¢

Goa was the first and final settlement in Portuguese India, from 1510 to 1962—more than 450 years. Coining began immediately, but no dates are available until the mid-1700s. Copper coins from that period bring $5 to $50; silver from $30 to $120 until the mid-1800s; gold, $200 up to $1,500. Modern mintage was introduced in 1870, producing variable values terminating with final decimal coinage. In December 1961, India took Goa, along with lesser Portuguese holdings, by military action, thus ending the four and one-half century regime.

HONG-KONG

Coins		Current Worth
1,000 Dollars	Gold (Obverse: portrait of Queen Elizabeth II)	$400 to $600

Coined annually, beginning with 1975 in honor of the Queen's visit, it carried the royal Coat-of-Arms on the reverse. Successive issues have carried the Chinese Year on the reverse, with appropriate symbols.

ISRAEL

New Coinage (1980)

Coins		Current Worth
500 Sheqalim	Gold	$500
25 Sheqalim	Gold	$ 50
10 Sheqalim	Copper-Nickel	$ 1.25
5 Sheqalim	Copper-Aluminum-Nickel	$ 1.25
1 Sheqel	Copper-Nickel	25¢
Half Sheqel	Copper-Nickel	15¢
10 New Agorot	Bronze	10¢
5 New Agorot	Aluminum	10¢
1 New Agorot	Aluminum	10¢

Coincident with the above issue, the following coins of a commemorative nature were also minted:

10 Sheqalim	Gold (2 types)	$350
2 Sheqalim	Silver (2 types)	$ 35
1 Sheqel	Silver	$ 25

JERSEY

New Coinage (1983)

Coins		Current Worth
1 Pound (British Royal Mint)	Nickel-Brass	$ 5

The following coins have been added to the Decimal System as listed on page 188: 50 New Pence; 10 New Pence; 5 New Pence; 1 New Penny; Half New Penny. All bear the legend NEW PENNY, but are the same in design and in metal as the corresponding "old" pence, and have approximately the same current value.

KAMPUCHEA

(Cambodian People's Republic)

Coins		Current Worth
100,000 Riels	Gold	$450
50,000 Riels (Two types)	Gold	$150
10,000 Riels (Two types)	Silver	$100
5,000 Riels (Two types)	Silver	$ 57.50

In 1970, the Kingdom of Cambodia became the Khmer Republic which lasted for five years. In 1974 the preceding coinage was minted. These were put on sale during 1976 by the new People's Democratic Republic of Kampuchea (the country's new name) but no steps were taken toward a circulating currency until the Riel was established at 25¢ (U.S. money) in December 1980, with coinage as a future prospect.

KIRIBATI

Coins		Current Worth
5 Dollars	Silver	$ 20
1 Dollar	Copper-Nickel	$ 4.50
50 Cents	Copper-Nickel	$ 3
25 Cents	Copper-Nickel	$ 1.75
10 Cents	Copper-Nickel	$ 1
5 Cents	Copper-Nickel	50¢
1 Cent	Bronze	15¢

Formerly known as the Gilbert Islands, part of a British crown colony in the South Pacific Ocean, Kiribati became an independent nation in 1979.

LAOS

(People's Democratic Republic)
New Coinage (1980)

Coins		Current Worth
50 Att	Aluminum	$ 1
20 Att	Aluminum	40¢
10 Att	Aluminum	20¢

In November, 1981, the new Kip (100 Att) was established at 10¢ (U.S. money).

LESOTHO

Coinage of 1979

Coins		Current Worth
1 Maloti	Copper-Nickel	$ 2
50 Liscente	Copper-Nickel	$ 1.50
25 Liscente	Copper-Nickel	$ 1.25
10 Liscente	Copper-Nickel	$ 1
5 Liscente	Nickel-Brass	75¢
2 Liscente	Nickel-Brass	50¢
1 Liscente	Nickel-Brass	25¢

Formerly Basutoland, a South African state under British protection since 1867. It became the Independent Kingdom of Lesotho in 1966.

MEXICO

Coinage of the 1980s

Coins		Current Worth
20 Pesos	Copper-Nickel	$ 1
10 Pesos	Copper-Nickel	75¢
5 Pesos	Copper-Nickel	50¢
1 Peso	Copper-Nickel	20¢
50 Centavos	Copper-Nickel	15¢
20 Centavos	Copper-Nickel	10¢
10 Centavos	Copper-Nickel	10¢

Bullion Issues
(Uncirculated)

1 Onza (ounce)	Gold	$400
Half Onza	Gold	$200
Quarter Onza	Gold	$100
1 Onza	Silver	$ 25

MOZAMBIQUE

Latest Coinage (1980)

Coins		Current Worth
20 Meticals	Copper-Nickel	$ 7.50
10 Meticals	Copper-Nickel	$ 4.50
5 Meticals	Aluminum	$ 2.50
2 1/2 Meticals	Aluminum	$ 1.75
1 Metical	Brass	$ 1
50 Centavos	Aluminum	65¢

NIGER

Coins		Current Worth
1000 Francs	Silver	$ 55
500 Francs	Silver	$ 35
100 Francs	Gold	$575
50 Francs	Gold	$300
25 Francs	Gold	$175
10 Francs	Gold	$100
5 Francs	Silver	$ 60

A former French colony in West Africa, the Republic of Niger declared its independence in 1960. The coins listed above have been issued *in proof only*.

SINGAPORE

Coinage Beginning in 1980

Coins		Current Worth
50 Dollars	Silver	$ 45
10 Dollars	Nickel	$ 9.50
5 Dollars	Copper-Nickel	$ 5.50

All coins from $50 down to 1¢ have been struck in *silver* as *proofs*. (See list of denominations on page 252).

SOMALIA

Higher Values

Coins		Current Worth
10 Shillings	Silver	Proof
10 Shillings	Copper-Nickel	$ 4
5 Shillings	Copper-Nickel	$ 2.50

Values of 1,500, 500, 200, 100, 50, 20 shillings have been struck in gold proof.

TOGO

Issued 1924–1956

Coins		Current Worth
5 Francs	Aluminum-Bronze	$ 3.50
2 Francs	Aluminum-Bronze	$ 5.50
2 Francs	Aluminum	$ 10
1 Franc	Aluminum-Bronze	$ 4.50
1 Franc	Aluminum	$ 9.50
50 Centimes	Aluminum-Bronze	$ 3.50

Coinage of Republic (1977)

50,000 Francs	Gold	$350
25,000 Francs	Gold	$250
15,000 Francs	Gold	$150
10,000 Francs	Silver	$ 55
5,000 Francs	Silver	$ 35
2,500 Francs	Silver	$ 25

Originally part of Togoland, a German colony in Africa, Togo was acquired by France after World War I and became an independent republic in 1960.

TOKELAU ISLANDS

Coins		Current Worth
1 Tala	Copper-Nickel 1978	$ 3.50
1 Tala	Copper-Nickel 1979	$ 3.50
1 Tala	Copper-Nickel 1980	$ 3.50
1 Tala	Copper-Nickel 1981	$ 3.50

Each coin in the series has a different reverse. All are available in *silver* as *proofs.*

These islands form a New Zealand territory north of Samoa in the South Pacific Ocean.

TUVALU

Coins		Current Worth
10 Dollars	Silver	$ 37.50
5 Dollars	Silver	$ 22.50
1 Dollar	Copper-Nickel	$ 3.50
50 Cents	Copper-Nickel	$ 1.50
20 Cents	Copper-Nickel	65¢
10 Cents	Copper-Nickel	35¢
5 Cents	Copper-Nickel	20¢
2 Cents	Bronze	10¢
1 Cent	Bronze	10¢

When the British colony of the Gilbert and Ellice Islands became independent in 1976, the Ellice group adopted the name of Tuvalu, also known as the Lagoon Islands. The group is located in the South Pacific Ocean.

WESTERN SAMOA

In addition to its regular coinage, Western Samoa struck nearly 20 types of one tala pieces in copper-nickel from 1969 to 1981—all related to famous people or notable events. All are obtainable at prices from $2 to $6.50 according to condition. About half of these were also struck in *silver* as *proofs* which have been sold at prices from $20 to $65 or higher.

VIETNAM

Coinage from 1975

Coins		Current Worth
1 Dong	Aluminum	$ 10
5 Hao	Aluminum	$ 3
2 Hao	Aluminum	$ 1.75
1 Hao	Aluminum	$ 1.50
5 Xu	Aluminum	$ 1
2 Xu	Aluminum	75¢
1 Xu	Aluminum	50¢

Other titles in the Fell Collector's Series: